I REMEMBER THAT!

Captivating Stories, Interesting Facts and Fun Trivia for Seniors

BILL O'NEILL

ISBN: 978-1-64845-078-5

TABLE OF CONTENTS

INTRODUCTION

Welcome to *Trivia for Seniors: Exciting Facts from the '50s, '60s, '70s, and '80s,* a fun book to challenge yourself on important historical events and personalities, pop culture, and the science and technology of the first four decades after World War II. For many of you reading this, those were your "glory years" when you were attending sock hops, getting groovy, or becoming a wolf of Wall Street. Yes, for many of the Baby Boomer generation, these were the greatest years for many different reasons.

You probably remember how scared you felt during the Cuban Missile Crisis, or how you were baffled when you first heard about the Internet. Were you an expert with the hula hoop? What was your favorite sitcom of the 1970s? Did you wait in a long line to see the first installment of the *Star Wars* franchise in 1977?

This book covers all these questions and more, helping to refresh your memory on some of the most important world events throughout your life, and introducing you to a few obscure ones that you may have overlooked.

Whether you were a kid growing up in the '50s, a college student in the '60s and '70s or trying to take over the financial world in the '80s, there's something in this book for you. So, okay Boomer, get off your couch, fire up your desktop, and test your knowledge of the most important decades of your life.

And non-Boomers, feel free to read the book as well. It'll be fun to match trivia wits with your parents and grandparents about their generation, and in the process, you may even learn a few things!

This book is divided into four chapters — a chapter for each of the decades — with each chapter subdivided into the topics of history, pop culture, and science. At the end of each topic/ subheading is a ten-point quiz for you to test your knowledge, and a "Did You Know?" section that provides five extra related factoids.

So, sit back, relax, and relive the greatest years of your life. You're guaranteed to have plenty of fun!

CHAPTER 1:

THE 1950S

1950s History

The Korean War

The 1950s are viewed by many as a kinder, gentler time in America, and even the world for that matter. And most of you Boomers who can remember it probably agree. With that said, when you get right down to it, though, there was quite a bit going on in the good ole US of A, and the world, in the '50s.

And the decade started with a bang…literally.

In 1948, when Korea was divided into the Democratic People's Republic in the north and the Republic of Korea in the south, conflict was bound to happen. North Korea was a communist regime and was supported by the Soviet Union and communist China, while South Korea was a democratic regime backed by the United States and its allies. It was the beginning of the Cold War, and something was bound to happen — and it did on June 25, 1950, when North Korea invaded South Korea.

The United Nations sent troops to fight the North Koreans, although it was primarily the United States, Australia, and South Korea that did most of the fighting.

The war was very bloody and brutal, especially when the Chinese joined in on North Korea's side. One of the bloodiest battles was the Battle of Chosin Reservoir from November 27 to December 14, 1950, during which the Americans lost more than 1,000 men to the Chinese and were forced to retreat.

The front lines constantly changed, sometimes by hundreds of miles at a time, and fighting took place along beaches, in the mountains, and the freezing cold and blistering heat. Finally, on July 27, 1953, an armistice was signed that ended the fighting and established the border between the two Koreas at the 38th Parallel - ironically, this was the border before the battle began!

More than 500,000 died on both sides, among them more than 45,000 Americans.

You may remember seeing some newsreel footage of the Korean War when you went to the Saturday matinee, or if your family had a little more money, you probably saw something about it on television.

For all of you Boomers, the Korean War set the tone for the next several decades, as it was the opening shot in the Cold War. It was a demonstration of how devastating modern wars could be in a short time in a very enclosed space.

The Death of a Dictator

On March 5, 1953, Joseph Stalin, the man who many consider the worst dictator of the 20th century, died. But you probably don't remember what you were doing on that day. As the dictator of the USSR/Soviet Union, Stalin tightly controlled the press and his Russia was a very tightly closed country, so when he died, it wasn't publicized until a day later, and even then, many people around the world doubted if it was true.

But it *was* true, and it marked the end of an era and a significant milestone in the Cold War.

Stalin was born Ioseb Besarionis dze Jughashvili on December 18, 1878, in the town of Gori, Georgia (the country not the state!). After becoming an avowed communist, he moved to Russia and changed his name to "Stalin - teel" in Russian - to better fit in among ethnic Russians. Stalin lived up to his name, becoming known for violent, thug tactics in the Communist Party in the early 1900s, while on his way to becoming the leader of the party and eventually the Soviet Union in 1924.

Stalin is best remembered for leading the Soviet Union to war on the one hand, and on the other hand, for imprisoning and killing millions of his political opponents before, during, and after the war. He is often cited as being responsible for the Ukrainian genocide known as the Holodomor in the early 1930s.

Brutal as he was, Stalin was able to hold on to power for nearly 30 years and developed a cult of personality that still exists in some parts of Russia.

If you can remember Stalin, it was probably due to his constant sabre rattling; or maybe his bushy moustache left a mark on your mind. Whatever you may remember about Stalin, it's largely the result of how important he was. His death rapidly changed the dynamics of the Cold War.

"I Like Ike"

Just months before Stalin died, another icon from World War II became the American president.

Dwight David Eisenhower was the Supreme Commander of the Allied forces in Europe during World War II and was viewed by many in the United States, and the world, as a stabilizing influence in a world on shaky ground.

The Cold War was a new phenomenon, and no one knew where it would go. When Eisenhower threw his hat in the presidential ring in 1952 as a Republican, the people overwhelmingly voted to put him in the nation's highest office.

Eisenhower was one of only six presidents never to have been elected to an office previously, but he didn't let that slow him down!

Just like the 1957 Bell Air Chevy that become an icon of the economic prosperity of the '50s, and the newly built Interstate Highways that they drove down, Eisenhower was a symbol of strength, stability, and American conservatism. On domestic issues, Eisenhower was a slightly liberal/progressive, using the government for programs such as the Interstate Highway System; keeping some of Roosevelt's programs; adding the Department of Health, Education, and Welfare to the government; and supporting desegregation.

But make no mistake, when it came to geopolitics, Eisenhower was a warrior.

Eisenhower planned to face communism wherever it cropped up and confront it by force if necessary. In an April 7, 1954, press conference, Eisenhower branded his policy of confronting communism as the "Domino Theory."

He described it in these words:

"You have a row of dominoes set up, you knock over the first one, and what will happen to the last one is the certainty that it will go over very quickly."

There's a good chance you remember Ike giving press conferences on television during the 1950s. If you don't remember his 'Falling Dominos' speech, you may recall one of his many other press conferences. Overall, Eisenhower gave more than 200 televised press conferences and was the first American president to realize the full potential of the medium.

In the end, Ike's policies proved to be successful. The economy and country were stable, and Americans were safe from the threat of a communist invasion. Ike was reelected in a landslide in 1956 that was almost as big as the one that put him in office in 1952. Eisenhower also understood modern political campaigns and that having a campaign slogan as simple as "I Like Ike" could pay big dividends.

Truly, the 1950s was Ike's decade, and even if you remember anything about the politics of it, Eisenhower is probably one of the first people that come to your mind.

They Called Him Mao

Do you remember the first time you heard the name Mao Zedong? Chances are, you probably giggled a little. It's not that there was anything funny about Mao Zedong - quite the opposite actually, as he was a brutal dictator - but his presence on the world scene was certainly different, to say the least.

But, before Mao, the Chinese hadn't made much of an impact on the world scene.

When Mao took power in China and proclaimed it a communist state on October 1, 1949, people around the world, and Americans in particular, didn't know what to think. Communism had been around for a while at that point, but the Soviet Union was the primary communist state so as exotic as the ideology was, it wasn't too exotic.

The Soviet Union was just Russia plus a number of smaller countries in Central Asia and Eastern Europe, so the people didn't look that much different from the average American or Western European at the time.

And outside Stalin, most of the Soviet leaders wore Western-style clothing. Yes, communism was weird and even abhorrent to most Americans, but it wasn't the weirdest thing ever.

China, though, was a land of mystery to most Americans in the 1950s. In fact, it was exotic to most people throughout the world. The average American knew a little about Japan from World War II but next to nothing about China. At least, nothing factual.

There China was at the start of the 1950s, the largest communist state in the world by population, ruled by a guy whose name most Westerners couldn't agree on how to spell and who always wore military uniforms.

Americans quickly learned who Mao was, though, when China fought on North Korea's side in the Korean War. I'm sure if you grew up after the Korean War, you remember your dad talking about Mao as he read about China in the newspaper, or perhaps his name came up at the dinner table.

And unlike the many Soviet dictators after Stalin, Mao was around for quite some time (1893-1976).

Revolt in Hungary

When World War II ended, the Allied forces met in Berlin, which meant that the Soviet forces were in control of most of Eastern Europe. The first thing they did was to establish various communist puppet governments in most of the countries.

Needless to say, the people in those countries weren't happy, but little was said or done while Stalin ran things in the USSR.

When Stalin died, though, many people in the communist countries of Poland, Czechoslovakia, Bulgaria, and Hungary hoped the next Soviet leader would ease up on their countries and allow them more autonomy. When Nikita Khrushchev became the next leader of the Soviet Union after Stalin died, many thought it was the time to make a move.

After all, Khrushchev seemed more open to dialogue and he wore Western-style clothing, so how bad could he be?

Well, as moderate as Khrushchev may have been, he was under immense pressure from communist hardliners to show he was tough. So, when the people of Hungary rose up in revolt against their communist government on June 23, 1956, he had to react.

Do you remember the news reports of the Hungarian Revolution? If you do, then images of young Hungarian men throwing Molotov cocktails at Soviet tanks may have been burned into your mind. The image became the international symbol of resistance to the Soviet Union, but it wasn't enough to stop the mighty Soviet Army.

On November 4, Khrushchev gave the order for more than 30,000 Soviet troops and 1,000 tanks to enter the Hungarian capital city of Budapest. The revolution was quickly suppressed, leaving more than 3,000 Hungarians and 700 Soviet soldiers dead. Another 200,000 Hungarians had to flee the land as refugees, with many ending up in the United States, Canada, and England.

The Soviets won that round in the Cold War, but there would be several more battles to come.

Crisis in Egypt

If you can remember 1956, then you probably remember it as being a tense time. The Hungarian Revolution had the real potential to be the start of World War III, and as that crisis was happening, another one began hundreds of miles to the south in Egypt.

The Suez Canal was built in the 1800s by the French to facilitate trade from Europe to Asia. It was administered jointly by the British and French until Egyptian military dictator Gamal Abdel Nasser nationalized the canal in July 1956.

The British responded by invading the canal zone along with the French and the fairly newly created state of Israel on October 29, 1956.

The Israeli forces advanced via land, while the British and French advanced by the sea and dropped paratroopers from the air.

The fighting was over by November 7, with more than 3,000 Egyptians dead and just under 200 killed on the British, French, and Israeli side. It may have been a tactical victory for the British, French, and Israelis; but it was a strategic victory for the Egyptians and Americans.

President Eisenhower negotiated a peace that gave the Americans prestige and allowed the Egyptians to save face by keeping control of the canal. The British and French got nothing except a diminished role in global politics.

The Israelis also came out ahead, demonstrating that they had a state-of-the-art military that could hang with the big boys.

In the end, Eisenhower's diplomacy prevented the Suez Crisis from becoming a full-blown war that could have sparked World War III.

1950s History Quiz

1. Who succeeded Joseph Stalin as the leader of the Soviet Union?

2. In what year was Dwight D. Eisenhower first elected US president?

3. Great Britain, France, and _____ attacked Egypt during the Suez Crisis.

4. North Korea and South Korea are separated at the _____ Parallel.

5. In 1956, most of the action in the Hungarian Revolution took place in what city?

6. What was the game that Eisenhower referred to in his famous "Falling" speech?

7. _____ was the leader of China during the Korean War.

8. In what country was Joseph Stalin born?

9. More than _____ Americans lost their lives in which Korean War battle that lasted from November 27 to December 15, 1950?

10._____ was the leader of Egypt during the Suez Crisis.

Answers

1. Nikita Khrushchev

2. 1952

3. Israel

4. 38th

5. Budapest

6. Dominos

7. Mao Zedong

8. Georgia

9. The Battle of Chosin Reservoir

10. Gamal Abdel Nasser

Did You Know?

- The United Kingdom (Great Britain), France, Belgium, the Netherlands, Luxembourg, the United States, Canada, Portugal, Norway, Italy, Denmark, and Iceland all signed onto the alliance that became known as the North Atlantic Treaty Organization or NATO on April 4, 1949. To counter this, the Soviet Union started an alliance of Eastern European communist states — Poland, Hungary, Czechoslovakia, Bulgaria, Romania, East Germany, and the Soviet Union — on May 14, 1955, known as the Warsaw Pact.

- The Domino Theory was later used to justify American involvement in the Vietnam War and US intervention in Latin America.

- Nikita Khrushchev was born in a small village on the Russian side of the Ukraine-Russian border in 1894, although his family was ethnic Ukrainians. He worked as a factory worker and labor organizer before serving with distinction in the Bolshevik army during the Russian Civil War (1917-1922).

- For much of the 1950s, the United States experienced its second "Red Scare." The Red Scare philosophy held that the US was under constant threat of a communist military invasion from the Soviet Union and/or China, which was being facilitated by communists and communist sympathizers in America. Wisconsin Senator Joseph McCarthy most notably led investigations and hearings on communists in the government, while the congressional House Un-American Activities Committee (HUAC) investigated communism in Hollywood and pop culture.

- Imre Nagy was the leader of Hungary during the Hungarian Revolution. Although he was a communist, he supported the revolt. Nagy was later arrested by the Soviets in Yugoslavia and returned to Hungary where he was tried in a secret court and executed in 1958.

1950s Pop Culture

Elvis the Pelvis

Do you remember when you first saw rock 'n' roll legend Elvis Presley sing and dance his way into the hearts of America and the world? Although Elvis had played several TV performances throughout 1956, which included singing his hit "Hound Dog" to a basset hound on the *Steve Allen Show*, I'm sure the one you remember is his September 9 appearance on the *Ed Sullivan Show*.

Due to Presley's performances on other shows, the word was out about his unique style that blended rhythm and blues with country and gospel. The most risqué aspect of Presley's live act at the time, though, was his dance moves. His unorthodox movements, especially his hip gyrations, caught the attention of teens across the country - and their parents, who often complained to TV stations.

It also earned him the moniker "Elvis the Pelvis."

So, when Elvis made his famous appearance on the *Ed Sullivan Show*, they only showed him from the waist up! If you "remember" him dancing around the stage, gyrating, it was either because you saw one of his pre-*Sullivan* performances, or one of his later ones from the '60s or '70s when the censors eased up.

That performance on *Sullivan* made Elvis a household name, a cultural icon, and synonymous with 1950s America. He became one of the top-selling artists of the 1950s, his songs were in every jukebox (we'll get to that in a bit), and boys everywhere attempted to emulate his look, with slicked-back "ducktail" haircuts, wing-tipped shoes, and flashy shirts.

Elvis also spawned a legion of musicians who attempted to copy, or were heavily influenced by, his style, which came to be known as "rockabilly."

And when Elvis was drafted in the US Army in 1958 for a two-year hitch, his popularity didn't wane thanks to the release of previously non-released singles.

Truly, if there's one person who epitomizes 1950s pop culture in America, it is none other than Elvis Aaron Presley, or as he was more widely known as, simply "Elvis."

"One of These Days, Alice!"

Those of you who can remember television in the 1950s know that it was vastly different from TV today. TVs in the '50s were big, bulky, and awfully expensive, relatively speaking, so chances are if you had a TV in your house when you were a kid, it was the only one. It's also likely that it was a common occurrence for neighbors to drop in to watch shows such as Ed Sullivan, where you possibly caught one of Elvis' early performances.

Or maybe you remember watching the *Honeymooners* starring Jackie Gleason as the boisterous bus driver, Ralph Kramden, who had plenty of bark with no bite. The *Honeymooners* began as a skit segment on various variety shows before becoming a regular show that ran from 1955 through 1956 on the CBS network.

It immediately became the first successful sitcom of its type in American television history, creating a template for sitcoms in the following decades. Unlike family shows that were on at the time, such as *Leave it to Beaver* and *Father Knows Best*, the *Honeymooners* was about working-class people in New York City with no children. It wasn't always pretty and would be considered politically incorrect by today's standards, but it was always funny!

Starring opposite Gleason was Audrey Meadows, who played Ralph's wife, Alice. In many ways, Alice was the typical '50s housewife, spending her days cooking and cleaning for her husband, but she was no wallflower. Whenever the boisterous Ralph blew up over something, which was usually multiple times in an episode, he often threatened Alice by stating, "One of these days, Alice," and "to the moon!", implying he'd hit her.

Alice would respond by giving him an amused look and simply say, "Shut up" in a Brooklyn accent.

The banter of Ralph and Alice was augmented by their upstairs neighbor friends, Ed and Trixie Norton, played by Art Carney and Joyce Randolph. Ed was a dimwitted but lovable sewer worker and Trixie was his devoted wife.

As reruns of the *Honeymooners* are still shown on retro TV networks and streaming services, there's little doubt that it will continue to be remembered as an important part of 1950s pop culture.

The Ten Commandments and Ben-Hur

If you were going to the movies in the 1950s, chances are that you saw at least one "sword-and-sandal" epic. As the name implies, these were films set in ancient times, where the main character had to overcome great odds, usually to claim a throne and a beautiful woman. Countless low-budget sword-and-sandal films were produced in Italy in the 1960s - most notably were dozens that centered on the exploits of the Greek hero Hercules - but it all began in the United States with two films in the 1950s: *The Ten Commandments* and *Ben-Hur*.

These were not only the two highest-grossing films of the 1950s, but they were also culturally important for several reasons.

The 1956 film *The Ten Commandments*, which told the story of the biblical Exodus, starred Charlton Hesston as Moses and Yul Brenner as Ramesses the Great. Filmed on location in Egypt, it was an immediate hit around the world and provided the top standard to which all later epics would be compared.

And it didn't take long for another epic to be produced.

Following on the success of *The Ten Commandments*, the 1959 movie *Ben-Hur* tells the fictional story of the titular character, who crosses paths with personalities such as Pontus Pilate and Jesus. Although filmed in Hollywood, the producers of *Ben-Hur* followed the pattern set by *The Ten Commandments* in most other ways, even by casting Charlton Heston in the lead role!

Although the winning formula *The Ten Commandments* and *Ben-Hur* were often copied in the following years and decades in similar films and quasi-remakes, none of those films had the lasting cultural impact as the originals.

Hula Hoops and Jukeboxes

The 1950s may have been low-tech compared to today, but that didn't stop you Boomers, from having plenty of fun as kids, did it? When you think back to all the fun you had as kids during the '50s, chances are if you're a woman, you remember playing with dollhouses and if you're a man, you dressed up like a cowboy or an Indian with your friends and siblings.

Or maybe you pretended you were Flash Gordon.

No iPods or tablets could be found in the hands of kids in the 1950s; instead, toyboxes full of Play-Doh, Silly Putty, Slinkies, dolls, toy guns, and farm sets were the norm.

The first Barbie dolls went on the shelves of stores in 1959, and the classic Matchbox cars began selling in 1953.

And no doubt you can remember the Hula Hoop, right?

In 1958, the Wham-O toy company began selling their plastic version of the centuries-old toy, making it synonymous with the 1950s in the process.

If you were a teen in the 1950s and had outgrown toys, you probably remember going to the soda fountain for a cherry Coke sundae and putting a handful of change into the jukebox to listen to Elvis. Although the jukebox had been around for a while before the 1950s, the Seeburg Corporation introduced a jukebox that could play small 45rpm records, which meant a machine could hold many more songs than before. After 1950, jukeboxes could be found just about anywhere where you could get a meal in the United States.

Jukeboxes of the 1950s could only carry about 100 songs per machine, which of course is a far cry from those of today.

Looking back, you probably chuckle to yourself when you think how easily amused you were by the relatively low-tech toys and gadgets that dominated the pop culture of the '50s.

But a part of you also misses those toys and that era, right?

Greasers

The United States and most industrialized countries were pretty homogeneous before World War II. The people in each country were overwhelmingly of the same ethnicity, practiced the same religion, and spoke the same language. There also wasn't much variety within the general population in terms of dress and musical tastes.

But that all started to change in the 1950s.

With the emergence of Elvis Presley and rock 'n' roll music, an entirely new subculture sprang up that was tough, rebellious, and all about people living life on their own terms. These were the greasers. The greasers weren't political like the subcultures of the 1960s, but they did challenge the status quo of 1950s polite American society in many ways.

Greasers were primarily Hispanic and White working-class youths who liked rock 'n' roll and doo-wop, and adopted a tough, street-smart look. Greaser guys wore their hair long (relatively speaking for the '50s) and often slicked it back with Vaseline or Brylcream into a "ducktail." They wore Levi jeans, leather or denim jackets, and tennis shoes or engineer boots. Greasers also liked to wear white t-shirts with a pack of cigarettes rolled up in the sleeve and a single smoke behind an ear.

And oh yeah, you can't forget the trusty switchblade that every true greaser carried!

As for the greaser girls, or greasettes, they liked plenty of make-up, tight pants, and big hair.

Although the vast majority of American youths were never even remotely involved with the greaser subculture, there's no denying the influence it had on American pop culture. The 1955 film *Blackboard Jungle* used greaser culture and doo-wop in what was at the time a controversial movie.

Elvis Presley also adopted a semi-greaser look when he rose to fame in the '50s, and who can forget the musical and film, *West Side Story*? In case you aren't familiar with it, *West Side Story* was about two greaser gangs - one White and one Puerto Rican - at war with each other over turf in 1950s New York City.

But as tough as the greasers were, they were just too much a part of the '50s, so by the beginning of the 1960s, the hardcore greasers graduated to more hardcore street gangs and biker gangs while the rest moved to the suburbs.

Baseball in California

Today, football is the most popular sport in the USA, but for most of American history, baseball had the honors. Baseball is still America's pastime and the game most identified with the country due to its continued, albeit slightly diminished popularity and history.

And back in the 1950s, there was no game more popular than baseball in America.

New York Yankee Mickey Mantle was about the most popular baseball player in America at the time - nearly every American boy dreamed of being just like Mantel, playing in front of a packed stadium. So, as the American population grew - when more and more of you Boomers were born - so too did the interest in baseball and the money behind it.

By the mid-1950s, the bigwigs in the National and American leagues as well as the owners, realized that baseball needed to expand to new territories, particularly to California.

California was experiencing a second gold rush of sorts in the 1950s, as droves of people flocked there to work in the booming entertainment, arms, and tech industries. California was awash with television and movie studios, companies that made planes, ships, and guns, several military bases, and some of the earliest tech companies.

California was also home to plenty of money and people in the 1950s.

So, since *all* Major League teams were located in Northeastern and Midwestern cities, and since *most* of those cities had an American League and a National League team, it was decided that some of the underperforming clubs would be moved out west.

The National League Boston Braves were the first team to move. They moved to Milwaukee in 1953, and then to Atlanta in 1966 and were renamed Milwaukee Braves.

The American League St. Louis Browns then moved to Baltimore in 1954 and became the Baltimore Orioles and the American League Philadelphia Athletics moved to Kansas City in 1954 before moving to Oakland, California in 1968.

But there's little doubt that the moves that made the biggest noise were when the National League's New York Giants and Brooklyn Dodgers left the Big Apple in 1957 for San Francisco and Los Angeles, respectively. The moves left New York with no

National League team until the Mets began playing in 1962, which left hardcore fans upset and bewildered.

Major League Baseball teams continued to move cities after the 1950s, but never again did they do so in such great numbers and such a short period.

1950s Pop Culture Quiz

1. In 1950, the _____ corporation introduced jukeboxes that could play 45rpm records.

2. Who was the lead actor in both *The Ten Commandments* and *Ben-Hur*?

3. What was the name of the actor who played Ralph Kramden in *The Honeymooners*?

4. The _____ moved from New York to San Francisco in 1957.

5. What song did Elvis Presley perform for a basset hound on live television in 1956?

6. What was one of the clothing signifiers of being a greaser?

7. In what year did the first Barbie dolls hit the shelves of stores?

8. Ralph Kramden's best friend was _____ on the *Honeymooners*.

9. What was the little road bump that could have impacted Elvis' career in the late '50s?

10. What happened to the St. Louis Browns?

Answers

1. Seeburg

2. Charlton Heston

3. Jackie Gleason

4. Giants

5. "Hound Dog"

6. For boys: Levi jeans; denim jacket; leather jacket; t-shirt with cigarette rolled up in the sleeves; engineer boots or sneaker; hair greased with Vaseline or Brylcream into a "ducktail." For girls: heavy make-up, tight pants, big hair.

7. 1959

8. Ed Norton

9. He was drafted into the Army in 1958

10. They moved to Baltimore and become the Orioles

Did You Know?

- The hit 1960s animated sitcom, *The Flintstones*, was basically a rip-off of or influenced by (depending on who you ask) the *Honeymooners*. Fred and Wilma Flintstone were based on Ralph and Alice Kramden, with Barney and Betty Rubble, clearly being cartoon versions of Ed and Trixie Norton.

- When the St. Louis Browns became the Baltimore Orioles, it wasn't the first time that Baltimore had had a team with that name. The original Baltimore Orioles began playing in the American League in 1901 but moved to New York in 1903 to become the Yankees. No wonder Orioles and Yankees fans hate each other so much!

- Although Memphis, Tennessee is the city most associated with Elvis Presley and is where he lived most of his life and died, he was born in Tupelo, Mississippi in 1935. He moved with his family to Memphis for better opportunities in 1948, and the rest is history!

- Silly Putty was, and still is, made primarily from silicone polymers. It first hit the market in 1949, but it took a couple of years for the strange "toy" to take off; the first televised commercial was in 1957 during an episode of the *Howdy Doody Show*.

- Greasers were pretty much an American phenomenon, although the Teddy Boys were a similar subculture in Britain during the 1950s.

1950s Science

The Kitchen Revolution

Of all the scientific advances of the 1950s, the ones that you may remember the most were those in the kitchen. In the 1940s, especially during World War II, an average kitchen would feature a sink, draining board, counter, a ventilated larder, and an icebox. Most iceboxes were literally that - a box where large blocks of ice were stored that would keep foods from spoiling.

The refrigerator was introduced in the 1920s, but it wasn't until the 1950s that most people could afford them. The '50s also saw the entry of large range-style ovens into the kitchen. Electric dishwashers also began to grace more and more homes in the 1950s, although they were still a luxury that most couldn't afford.

Speaking of washing, automatic washing machines also surged in availability in the 1950s. The General Electric company introduced its first top-loading washing machine model in 1947, after which several other companies entered the washing machine fray. A big step forward in washing machine technology took place in 1957 when Winston Shelton and Gresham Jennings invented an electromechanical timer that put the washer through the cycles.

The automatic clothes dryer also became popular in the 1950s, although it was first invented in the 1930s and marketed in the 1940s.

Finally, the technology of air conditioning also made homes much cooler and more comfortable in the 1950s. Air conditioning was invented at several different points by many different people, but by the late 1940s, it was being sold commercially. By 1953, one million air conditioning units were in American homes, and by the end of the decade, that number had grown considerably.

Truly, the 1950s was the decade when convenience and technology first converged in the home to create what many remember as an era of domestic bliss!

Connecting the Country

Perhaps the biggest scientific advancement of the 1950s was one that brought together politics, economics, and engineering to produce something that many Americans today take for granted - The Interstate Highway system. Interstate highways are in every state (even Alaska and Hawaii, but don't ask me how you can technically have an "inter" state highway in a state that isn't connected to other states), helping to make driving time over long distances, or commutes to work, quicker and more efficient.

Yes, it's hard to imagine what life would be like without the Interstate system, given a quarter of all vehicle traffic in the US uses the Interstate Highway system's 48,440 miles of road.

So, how did the Interstate system come about?

Well, as the United States was growing, the old highway system was antiquated and unable to keep up and efficiently supply the country. More importantly, the threat of the Soviet Union and China meant that a method of moving troops quickly had to be devised.

How would the military get troops from the West Coast if the East Coast was attacked, and vice versa?

The idea for the Interstate system happened when President Eisenhower was still General Eisenhower in World War II. He saw how efficient the German Autobahn freeway system was, so he thought it could be replicated in the United States. There already were some freeways (limited access four-lane highways) in

America, but most were in the northeast and major urban centers.

Eisenhower envisioned freeways spread out like cobwebs across the country, connecting every state in the far-flung country.

The idea was pitched to Congress, which agreed to fund the project as the Federal Aid Highway Act of 1956.

The US Interstate Highway System continues to expand and is considered by many to be one of the world's most underrated engineering marvels. Chances are, if you went with your family on a trip in the 1950s and you had a chance to travel on one of the newly built roads, you also marveled at how different it was compared to traveling on a standard two-lane highway.

Music on the Go

You've probably already noticed that 1950s technology involved high-tech ideas (relatively speaking, of course) meeting convenience. The tech of the '50s was all about using new inventions and ideas to make the economy more efficient and to make people's lives a bit easier.

The new technologies of the '50s also made things *sound* a lot better.

As you watch your kids or grandkids listening to MP3s on their iPods, or as you listen to your favorite Boomer playlist on your device, it's amazing to think that it all began in 1954 with a small transistor radio called the Regency TR-1.

Receiver-only transistor radios had been in use by the military for a few years by the early 1950s, but the executives and engineers at Texas Instruments wanted to create a small, hand-held device that could be sold to the general public.

And at $49.95, the American-made Regency TR-1 wasn't cheap (optional earpiece was $7.50), but it was popular, selling 150,000 units. The TR-1 measured 3"x5"x1.25" - curiously about the size of current iPhones - ran on a Texas Instrument NPN transistor and was powered by a 22.5-volt battery.

The success of the Regency TR-1 spawned an entirely new market for portable radios that used transistor technology and helped catapult Texas Instruments to its status as one of the top tech companies in the world for more than three decades.

Defeating Polio

Poliomyelitis, better known as "polio," is a virus that affects the nervous system and muscles of those infected. Polio can cause paralysis, deformed limbs, and death among those afflicted with it, especially the young. And by the early 20th century, it was primarily children who were dying from it around the world, so some of the leading doctors and scientists began working on a vaccine.

But as experts raced to create a vaccine, more and more children died. There were considerable outbreaks of polio in the United States during the early '50s. If you can remember those times, you were no doubt confused and scared. Depending on the state, county, and/or city, families with a member who contracted polio were often quarantined. And I'm not talking about the COVID-19 style quarantines of today; no, these quarantines meant that people couldn't come or go from their homes at all. Groceries and other essentials had to be left at the door!

The number of deaths peaked at 3,200 in 1952 (if you think those numbers aren't remarkably high, take into consideration that the total population of the US was just over 163 million that year), creating a greater sense of urgency among researchers.

Finally, in 1952, researcher Jonas Salk developed the first effective polio vaccine. Testing began in 1953, and in 1955, mass vaccinations of children began, largely funded by the March of Dimes organization.

By the early 1960s, polio was no longer a concern in the United States, and its deadly reach had also diminished worldwide. The effective defeat of polio was utterly amazing, but even more amazing is how quickly it happened.

If you grew up in the '50s, then you probably recall hearing about the quarantines and feeling the fear, or maybe you were even quarantined or contracted the virus yourself. However, if you grew up only a few years later in the '60s, then polio likely played little to no role in your life.

The evolution of technology was truly taking place at breakneck speeds and was even going on in outer space!

Sputnik

Do you remember what you were doing on October 4, 1957, when the Soviet Union announced they had successfully launched the world's first artificial satellite, Sputnik 1, into orbit?

There's a good chance your parents were freaking out when they heard the news!

In fact, a lot of Americans were freaking out when they heard the news. "Now that the commies have satellites up there, how long until they put 'the bomb' up there?" That was the question most people asked.

For many people, it seemed like suddenly Flash Gordon and all the other 1950s sci-fi movies and comic books (that was another big part of 1950s pop culture, by the way) were coming true.

The Soviets followed that feat up by shooting the first animal, a dog named Laika, into space on November 3, 1957. Due to the limitations on space travel technology of the period, it was a one-way trip for the poor pooch, but the heroic dog's journey, along with Sputnik, helped set off the "space race."

The Americans responded by building their own space program and by the 1960s both sides were competing to explore and even colonize space. The space race of the '50s and '60s, though, actually began during World War II.

It was just before World War II that German scientists began building some of the world's first jets and as the war commenced, they invented the first rockets.

When the war was over, it was a race between the Soviets and Americans to grab as many of the German rocket scientists as they could, and by the 1950s, both sides had burgeoning space programs.

The Soviet Union had the initial advantage in the 1950s, scaring plenty of people in the Heartland in the process, but the Americans quickly caught up in the '60s.

Another Victory for Convenience

As 1950s technology became more and more centered on convenience and domestic consumption, it should be no surprise that one of the greatest - although often overlooked — inventions of the decade was the alkaline battery.

In case you're wondering, alkaline batteries are the majority of batteries that still power many devices such as flashlights, remote controls, and yes, radios.

People have experimented with different types of batteries throughout history, but it was the invention of the lead-acid battery in the 1800s that really propelled knowledge of energy storage technology. Lead-acid batteries proved to be quite effective, and are still used in cars today, but can you imagine having to lug a car battery around just to listen to a transistor radio? Neither could scientists, so they began developing smaller batteries in the early 1900s.

Nickel-cadmium and nickel-iron batteries that used an alkaline electrolyte were invented in the late 1800s and early 1900s. By the 1950s, consumer batteries were zinc-carbon dry cells, which - without getting too technical — meant that they worked but not for long.

Batteries back then didn't last very long, which was a good thing for battery companies, but not for the companies that made gadgets. Who'd want to buy their products if they cost more in batteries, right?

Well, in 1955 Canadian engineer Lewis Urry came up with a new battery invention that combined the size and convenience of zinc-carbon batteries on the market with the large, expensive alkaline batteries of the era. The result was the relatively long-lasting alkaline batteries of today.

The new battery was comprised of a manganese dioxide cathode, a powdered zinc anode, with an alkaline electrolyte. Urry's batteries hit the market in 1959, and before too long, teens across the world didn't have to get new batteries every week for their transistor radios.

The kids were sure happy, although maybe not so much their parents!

1950s Science Quiz

1. The Interstate Highway System came about during the presidency of _____.

2. The first effective polio vaccine was developed in what year?

3. In 1957, the Soviet Union launched _____ as the first artificial satellite and then one month later a dog named _____ became the first animal in space.

4. Consumer alkaline batteries hit the market in what year?

5. What company made the transistors for the first transistor radio available to consumers?

6. Name one of the inventors of the electromechanical timer that puts the washing machine into a cycle.

7. The Regency TR-1 radio was retailed for what price?

8. How many people died from polio in the United States in 1952?

9. What was the problem with alkaline batteries before Urry's invention?

10._____ of the country was the original purpose of the US Interstate Highway System.

Answers

1. Eisenhower

2. 1952

3. Sputnik; Laika

4. 1959

5. Texas Instruments

6. Winston Shelton or Gresham Jennings

7. $49.95

8. 3,200

9. They were too big to be portable

10. National defense

Did You Know?

- The first transistor was invented by the team of William Shockley, Walter Houser Brattain, and John Bardeen at Bell Laboratories in 1947. The trio's discovery not only led to the commercial development of the transistor radio, but they are also often considered the fathers of the Silicon Valley tech industry.

- The term vaccine is derived from the use of cow pox to vaccinate against smallpox. The word *vacca* is Latin for "cow."

- The National Aeronautics and Space Administration was officially organized by the United States government in 1958.

- The Interstate Highway system uses a standard system to name all its highways. Odd numbers are given for north-south interstates, and even numbers are given for east-west routes. Interstates that have three numbers are either a spur off a major interstate if they begin in an odd number (380), or a loop around a city if even (494).

- Laika was a stray female mutt found wandering on the streets of Moscow. She was described as an incredibly docile dog and worked well with researchers. One of the researchers brought her to his home to play with his children just before her fateful flight into the stars. It's believed Laika lived five to seven hours before succumbing to the elements. Laika's satellite crashed to earth five months later.

CHAPTER 2:

THE 1960S

1960s History

Berlin Divided

As the calendar rolled over from 1959 to the 1960s, there was plenty in store for the world in what turned out to be a turbulent decade. Things may have seemed quite placid in the first few years of the decade, and if you were a kid back then you probably remember it as such, but just beneath the surface was a whole lot of tension brewing between the Soviet Union and the United States.

And Berlin, Germany was ground zero of the conflict in 1961.

If you'll remember, when World War II ended, Joseph Stalin and the Soviet Union took control of Eastern Europe, making those countries communist in the process. Germany was occupied by all the major Allied forces, but Stalin wanted it for himself, particularly the capital city of Berlin.

So, Stalin surrounded US-occupied West Berlin with tanks and cut it off from the outside world. The Allies responded with the Berlin Airlift, which lasted for 323 days from June 1948 to May 1949. Stalin backed down and allowed West Berlin to stay free. East and West Germany officially separated that year as well, with East Germany becoming communist.

But the fight over Berlin was not over.

The communists still wanted to control what had become the city of West Berlin, which was essentially a free city in a sea of communist dictatorships.

In early 1961, Soviet leader Nikita Khrushchev thought he'd test the recently-elected - and in his estimation, quite inexperienced - President, John F. Kennedy. Soviet tanks were sent to the East Berlin-West Berlin border checkpoint known as "Checkpoint Charlie" on June 4, 1961. Kennedy responded by sending American tanks to greet them.

After a tense standoff of more than two months, the communists began building the Berlin Wall on August 13, 1961.

Kennedy successfully stood up for himself, West Berlin, democracy, and the American people, but he would face even bigger challenges from communist dictators, most of which came from south of the border.

Fidel, Fidel

If you remember the early '60s well, then you'll recall that America's biggest boogeyman at that time wasn't Khrushchev, it was Fidel Castro. And in many ways, Fidel Castro came from the central casting of Latin American despots.

> Beard — check!
> Aviator sunglasses — check!
> Cigar — check!
> And most importantly, military fatigues at all times — check!

Yes, Castro fitted nearly everyone's image of a tinpot dictator at the time, but he was no joke. He almost caused World War III!

Castro was a leftist who came to power when he and his merry band of revolutionaries, who were also led by the famous Che Guevarra, overthrew the corrupt right-wing dictator Fulgencio Batista in 1959. Eisenhower and the Americans weren't necessarily sad to see Batista go, but it didn't take Castro long to start cozying up to the Soviets.

And then Kennedy was elected.

Like Khrushchev, Castro thought he'd see what he could get away with by pushing Kennedy, although the American president also gave back his share to the Cuban dictator.

The first challenge took place on April 17, 1961, when CIA-trained Cuban exiles attempted to invade Cuba at the Bay of Pigs. The "Bay of Pigs Invasion," as it came to be known, was a disaster for the exiles, CIA, and Kennedy, as the Cuban army had completely suppressed it by April 20.

Then it was Castro's turn to make a move.

As the conflict between Kennedy and Castro was heating up, Khrushchev stepped in and convinced his communist buddy to let the Soviets build some nuclear missile silos on Cuba. After an American U-2 spy plane took photos of the construction in October 1962, President Kennedy interrupted all television programming (TV was still a fairly new medium for US presidents to use) on October 22 and told the American people what was happening, in no uncertain terms.

Kennedy blockaded Cuba with a naval task force and ordered any Cuban or Soviet attempts to circumvent the blockade to be attacked. The president stated that the US would further escalate with combined tactical nuclear strikes and a conventional military invasion of Cuba.

The Soviets would have responded with Intercontinental Ballistic Missiles (ICBMs) aimed at the USA and the Americans would have shot theirs at the USSR.

The world waited tensely to see what Castro and Khrushchev were going to do. People who lived through that period describe the tension as so thick it could be cut with a knife.

Finally, on October 28, Khrushchev backed down by agreeing to dismantle the nuclear missile sites in Cuba. Kennedy agreed to dismantle American nuclear capabilities in Turkey and Italy and to essentially leave Castro and Cuba alone. The Cuban Missile Crisis was the last time Castro played a major role in the Cold War, but it wouldn't be the last time the Americans and Soviets almost went to war.

Tragedy Strikes America

The Cuban Missile Crisis could have been the ultimate tragedy for the world, but it ended up being a great victory for Kennedy and his legacy. As a result, Kennedy enjoyed a great popularity boost at home and leaders abroad began to respect the young president.

The American economy was also doing well and the domestic problems that took hold later in the decade were not yet an issue. Kennedy's presidency seemed like the beginning of a new era, leading many to call it 'Camelot' just like the legendary King Arthur's court.

But then on November 22, 1963, at 12:30 pm central time, tragedy struck when Kennedy was assassinated by Lee Harvey Oswald.

You no doubt remember what you were doing when you learned the awful news. Schools were closed, businesses shut down, and police departments were put on high alert. No one knew what was happening. Was it the beginning of a communist invasion? Was it the work of a crazy person?

Oswald, who was a militant communist who lived in the Soviet Union for a while, was the only person ever implicated in the assassination, and he was himself assassinated by a sleazy nightclub owner named Jack Ruby. There are so many unanswered questions about the Kennedy assassination, and so many rabbit holes to go down, that it's impossible to say for sure at this point who, and how many people were involved.

What is known, though, is that those who's thought that Kennedy's presidency would mark the beginning of a new era were partially correct; Kennedy's violent *death* actually marked the end of the innocence of the '50s and the beginning of the turbulent '60s.

After Kennedy, things got a whole lot crazier in the '60s!

Where Is Vietnam?

"Where is Vietnam?" was a question you probably heard, or asked yourself, during the 1960s. The question isn't necessarily an indictment on the American educational system, which was regarded much more highly in the '60s than today, or on the nation of Vietnam's importance in the world. The reality is, though, that Vietnam was a small and relatively new country in the 1960s.

Vietnam was part of the French colony of Indochina until the French abandoned it in the 1950s, so many Americans still probably knew it as Indochina in the 1960s.

So, you're probably wondering, "When did the Vietnam War actually begin?"

Well, since the war was never declared, there wasn't any exact point when it began. President Eisenhower began sending military advisors there in the '50s as part of his Falling Dominos strategy, but it wasn't until Lyndon B. Johnson became president in 1963 (after Kennedy was assassinated) that American involvement ramped up.

After North Vietnamese ships allegedly fired on American ships in the Gulf of Tonkin in 1964, Johnson sent wave after wave of Americans into the southeast Asian country. Of course, the war led to much turmoil at home in America.

Civil Rights and Counterculture

By the mid-1960s, a sea of change had overtaken the United States and many other countries in the Western world. The US Supreme Court ruling, *Brown v. Board of Education* in 1954, ordered that the states had to end racial segregation in public schools. The ruling prompted Martin Luther King Junior and other Black leaders to organize protests against leaders of primarily Southern states that continued to enforce segregation.

Eventually, King's efforts paid off in the form of several bills passed by the US Congress and signed into law by President Johnson.

The Civil Rights Act of 1964 outlawed discrimination and segregation, while the Voting Rights Act of 1965 outlawed laws in many Southern states that prevented Blacks from voting. The Civil Rights Act of 1968 furthered these new laws.

Much of the Civil Rights Movement was peaceful, but there were some radicals — such as Stokely Carmichael, Huey Newton, the Black Panthers, and several other militant organizations - who used violence to forward their goals. These groups, who were termed "black power" and made the raised black fist popular, were often joined by young White leftists.

The Vietnam War was the catalyst for rebellion in the 1960s, which primarily came from college-age and educated young people from the suburbs and urban areas. With that said, though, most young people weren't involved in the anti-war movement.

The most prominent of the involved groups in the '60s was the Students for a Democratic Society (SDS), from which even more radical groups such as the Weather Underground were born. The American anti-war movement also became the basis on which the "counter-culture" was formed, where hippies and others decided to light up and drop out rather than take part in the system.

We'll get to them in a little bit.

The leaders of these anti-war groups, like Tom Hayden and Bill Ayers, who professed allegiance to communism, claimed to fight for the working man and income equality, often while living on trust funds and the largesse of their wealthy families. With plenty of money and time on their hands, these trust fund revolutionaries were able to travel extensively to start protests, riots, and sometimes even bombings.

The culmination of their work and some would say, the entire decade, came during the Democrat Party's national convention in Chicago in 1968.

A Tough Election

When thousands of SDS members showed up in Chicago on August 24, 1968, to protest at the

Democrat Party convention, it was a sign of how fractured the Democrat Party and the country were.

SDS rioted off and on for five nights in some of the parks and on the streets of Chicago but weren't able to affect the convention. The party faithful chose Hubert H. Humphrey as their candidate over the more liberal Eugene McCarthy. The Republican incumbent was Republican Richard M. Nixon.

As crazy as the SDS riots were outside the Democrat convention, it was only a sign of how crazy things had gotten that year overall. Popular Senator Robert Kennedy, who was the Democrat frontrunner, had been assassinated in June of that year, which placed the Democrats' hopes up in the air.

But their hopes were heightened slightly when segregationist-populist George Wallace ran as a third-party candidate, capturing the deep South states in the general election. Many in the Democrat Party had hoped that Wallace, who was an old-school segregationist Democrat, would peel votes away from Nixon, as more and more Southern votes were by then voting Republican.

Wallace wasn't enough to give the election to Humphrey, though. Nixon won 301 electoral votes to Humphrey's 191 and Wallace's 46. The popular vote was much closer, with Nixon only beating Humphrey by just over 500,000 votes and winning only 43.4% of the total. It was one of the most hotly contested and controversial elections in American history.

Well, until recently.

1960s History Quiz

1. Students for a _____ Society was the major left-wing student organization of the 1960s.

2. Vietnam was part of what French colony?

3. Who was the third-party candidate who tried to play "spoiler" in the 1968 US presidential election?

4. Construction on the Berlin Wall began in what year?

5. What year was the Voting Rights Act passed?

6. _____ and _____ were considered Black radicals in the 1960s.

7. John F. Kennedy's presidency was sometimes compared to what legendary/mythical royal court?

8. Where was the American Democrat Party's 1968 party convention held?

9. The Cuban Missile Crisis ended when President Kennedy did what?

10. What type of airplane took pictures of the Soviets installing nuclear missile silos in Cuba?

Answers

1. Democratic

2. Indochina

3. George Wallace

4. 1961

5. 1965

6. Huey Newton, Stokely Carmichael, the Black Panthers

7. Camelot

8. Chicago

9. Blockaded Cuba with the US Navy; threatened to invade Cuba

10. U-2

Did You Know?

- Bobby Seale, Angela Davis, Malcolm X, and Eldridge Cleaver were also notable Black militants/radicals in the 1960s. Although the exact origins of the term "black power" will probably never be known, Carmichael made it popular.

- SDS and its affiliated groups, including the Black Panthers, are generally considered by historians and political scientists to be part of the "New Left." By the 1990s, many of the New Left radicals had gone mainstream, with some, such as Bill Ayers, even having friends in the highest levels of the US government.

- Lee Harvey Oswald officially defected to the Soviet Union in October 1959, where he lived until June 1962. Oswald was not only allowed to return to the United States with no legal problems, but he was also given a repatriation loan of $435.71 to use with his wife Marina and their newborn daughter. The ease with which the US government treated Oswald during the height of the Cold War keeps the conspiracy theories going.

- The US military spent most of the Vietnam War fighting the guerrilla Vietcong (VC) army in South Vietnam and occasionally fighting off advances from the North Vietnamese Army from North Vietnam. From January 30 to September 23, 1968, the Vietcong carried out a massive three-wave guerilla campaign on American and South Vietnamese forces known as the Tet Offensive, for the Vietnamese New Year festival of Tet. Although it's considered a tactical victory for the South Vietnamese and the Americans, it was a strategic victory for the VC, who proved they could strike anywhere, at any time.

- In 1968, political party alignment was beginning but was still not complete. Most hardcore southern Democrats supported Wallace, but in the next presidential election, most of those voters began supporting the Republicans. In the North, many of the more socially liberal Republicans, who supported the Civil Rights actions switched over to the Democrats after 1968.

1960 Pop Culture

From Bonanza to Gunsmoke

If you remember television in the early to mid-1960s in America, chances are Westerns make up a large part of those memories. Whether it was James Arness and Ken Curtiss in *Gunsmoke*, Lorne Green and Michael Landon on *Bonanza*, or Chuck Connors on *The* Rifleman, you probably had your favorite Western and your favorite Western actors.

Although Western films had been made for some time before the '60s, it wasn't until the mid-'50s that the genre hit its stride (pun intended!) on the small screen. By 1960, there were 30 Westerns on primetime, which when you consider that this was long before cable, means that *most* shows on primetime were Westerns.

The shows were typically pretty formulaic, with the good guys almost always triumphing, although, for the shows that made it into the late 1960s, darker themes became more common, and the good guy didn't always win!

If you go back and watch some of these shows, in any given episode, you'll notice that the guest stars are a veritable who's who of actors from the era. Some actors even got their starts in starring roles. Clint Eastwood played the lead role on *Rawhide* during its run from 1959 to 1966, and the late Steve McQueen also began his career in small screen Westerns, namely in his role as a bounty hunter on *Wanted Dead or Alive*.

By the late 1960s, TV tastes, attitudes, and demographics had changed. The Westerns that continued to be successful had to adapt to the times to stay on the air, and while most didn't, a few did. *The Wild Wild West* first hit the air in 1965 and ran through 1969. It was successful because instead of being a standard Western, it borrowed elements from other popular TV genres of the late '60s, particularly spy and sci-fi shows. The main character, James West, played by Robert Conrad, was a spy who used all kinds of sci-fi equipment and faced super-criminals who had even more advanced weapons.

By the time, the '60s were over, though, so too was the era of the TV Westerns. In 1970, TV executives axed most of the remaining Westerns in what is known as the "rural purge," when the major networks got rid of "country" programming in favor of more urban-themed shows.

The British Invasion

Although rock 'n' roll was born in the USA, it became popular with legions of young fans around the world: from Europe to Australia, and from Latin America to Asia - anywhere where there was a jukebox, kids, record stores, and radio stations willing to play the music, there were young rock 'n' roll fans. And perhaps in no place outside the US was rock 'n' roll more popular than in Britain.

In 1964, British rock bands such as The Yardbirds, the Rolling Stones, the Animals, and of course, The Beatles were ready to jump across the Pond and try their luck in the birthplace of rock 'n' roll.

So began the famous "British Invasion."

If there was an exact time and place when the British Invasion began, it was February 9, 1964, in New York City. It was on that night that the Beatles performed on *The Ed Sullivan Show*, and just as Ed Sullivan had made Elvis a household name ten years earlier, he also made Americans familiar with the long-haired lads (at the time their hair was considered long) from Liverpool.

Hippies, Yippies, and Dropouts

We talked a little bit about the whole counter-culture movement that took place in the late '60s as part of the anti-war movement, but there was really a lot more to it than that. Young people who grew their hair long, who took illicit drugs and practiced "free love" were generally considered "hippies" in the '60s. Some were politically associated with New Left groups, but most just wanted to "drop out" of society.

And some were even more on the right-wing of the political spectrum.

The 1960s spawned a variety of biker gangs that were considered dropouts at the time, and many of those bikers often ran in the same circles as hippies. But make no mistake about it, bikers were never very sympathetic to the SDS/leftist message. There were even some events where members of the Hells Angels motorcycle gang clashed with anti-war protesters.

And if this smorgasbord of counterculture wasn't crazy enough, you may also remember a group called the "Yippies."

The Yippies were founded and led by radical leftist Abbie Hoffman, who was depicted in a scene in the movie *Forest Gump* on a stage wearing an American flag shirt. The Yippies are best remembered for pulling several pranks in the late '60s, including running a pig for the president of the US!

Truly, the '60s was a crazy time of turmoil and change and if you were a kid growing up during this period, it was all probably quite confusing. If you were in the middle of it, well, let's just say you probably had plenty of fun…from what you can remember!

Do You Think the Beehive Will Make a Comeback?

You probably heard the expression, "The more things change, the more they stay the same." Well, with fashion trends that certainly seems to be the case as much of what goes around definitely seems to come back around. And when it comes to the 1960s, there are some trends that have made comebacks, while others - well, I think most people hope they don't.

In terms of 1960s fashion, it's important to look at the decade as having two very distinct halves. In the early to mid-60s, women started wearing pants, particularly plaid, capri-style pants, and men and women both wore their jeans tight and skinny.

As you know, both of those styles have made recent comebacks.

After the British Invasion, trends quickly changed again, with hair getting longer for men and women, skirts getting shorter for women (the miniskirt), and Roman-style sandals becoming cool.

And who can forget go-go boots? They've also made a bit of a comeback in recent years.

By the late '60s, people were rocking bell-bottom pants, although those didn't really become mainstream until the 1970s.

Also, by the late '60s, the mop haircut was popular with young White men, while the conk - an artificially straightened short haircut - was popular with Black men.

Then there was the beehive!

Nearly every woman, no matter her ethnicity, rocked a beehive at some point during the decade. If you're a woman reading this and were an adult during the '60s, you can surely attest to this fact.

All of the major female music groups of the early to mid-'60s sported beehives and of course, there were the women of *Star Trek* as well! Many of these styles have made comebacks in recent years, and some women have worn beehives here and there since the '60s. Still, it remains to be seen if the beehive will ever make a serious comeback.

Should it?

The First Super Bowl

Most of you Boomer's love gridiron football, or simply "football" as it's called in the US and Canada. It's certainly become an American tradition and pretty much a holiday for most Americans to spend "Super Bowl Sunday" with friends and family watching the game, eating lots of junk food, and often consuming copious amounts of alcohol.

It's no wonder that the Monday after the Super Bowl is one of the biggest days for job absenteeism in the US.

The Super Bowl has also grown in worldwide significance, being broadcast to nearly every country, so people from all over the world can now sit down and watch the curious American sport once every year.

And it all began in the glorious '60s!

The first Super Bowl was played on January 15, 1967, between the Green Bay Packers and the Kansas City

Chiefs at the Los Angeles Memorial Coliseum in Los Angeles, California. The Packers won the game 35-10 in front of a crowd of nearly 62,000 people. The game was broadcast live across the nation and was a big hit.

But it was called the AFL-NFL Championship Game…huh?

When the first Super Bowl was played, the American Football League and the National Football League were separate leagues. The championship game was for bragging rights since the teams didn't play each other during the regular season. The Super Bowl name wasn't used until the third championship.

It's believed that the Kansas City Chief's owner, Lamar Hunt, came up with the name "Super Bowl." Although the name was apparently not popular at first, it eventually caught on and is now a standard part of the American lexicon.

Today, it'd be hard to find someone in the US who doesn't know what the Super Bowl is.

TV Ends the Decade in Space

The big trend on TV in the early '60s may have been the very low-tech genre of Westerns, but by the latter part of the decade, the high-tech genre of sci-fi was taking over. Although sci-fi was born in many ways in the '50s, along with the Space Race, it wasn't until the '60s when a big push was made to put space on the small screen.

Of course, the show that first comes to mind for most people is the original *Star Trek*, which ran from 1966-1969. Despite spawning five more series, several films, more films based on the later series, and recent film reboots of the original films, *Star Trek* was never very popular at the time, usually only rating in the middle of all the shows on television.

Some think that initial *Star Trek's* lack of initial success was due to its more cerebral plots, but it may have been related to the competition more than anything.

The sci-fi explosion began just as the TV Westerns were peaking.

The '60s began with the black-and-white *Twilight Zone* and *Outer Limits* series, and by the middle of the decade, most shows were being done in color.

And no director affected the course of 1960s American TV more than Irwin Allen.

First, there was *Voyage to the Bottom of the Sea* (1964-1968): the story about a top-secret nuclear sub that battled everything from ghosts to communists to aliens to keep America safe. Then there was the show about two time-traveling government agents called the *Time Tunnel* (1966-1967). The weirdest of all of Allen's shows was *The Land of the Giants* (1968-1970), which was about a group of hapless Earthlings who end up on a planet full of 50-foot-tall people.

But most of you reading this probably have the fondest memories of Allen's most popular show, *Lost in Space* (1965-1968). As cheesy as the plots and special effects look now, it still resonates on some level. Perhaps it's the family dynamic you rarely see today, or maybe it's the blend of comedy and sci-fi.

Whatever it was, you can still find *Lost in Space*, and most of the '60s sci-fi shows, on rerun channels and/or streaming services, demonstrating that some things never get old.

1960s Pop Culture Quiz

1. What was the unique '60s TV show that was part Western, part sci-fi, and part spy show?

2. The _____ were a radical leftist subculture started by Abie Hoffman.

3. What two teams played in the first Super Bowl?

4. This A-list film star got his start on the '60s Western TV show, *Rawhide*.

5. The British Invasion officially began when the Beatles appeared on what TV show?

6. What was a unique hairstyle worn by men in the '60s?

7. The so-called _____ purge is part of what ended the era of American TV Westerns.

8. Women liked to rock these boots in the '60s, and they've since made a bit of a comeback.

9. What biker club/gang sometimes clashed with radical leftists in the '60s?

10. _____ was a black-and-white sci-fi show that was on TV in the early 1960s.

Answers

1. *The Wild Wild West*

2. Yippies/Youth International Party

3. Green Bay Packers and Kansas City Chiefs

4. Clint Eastwood

5. *The Ed Sullivan Show*

6. Mop; Conk

7. Rural

8. Go Go

9. Hells Angels

10. *The Twilight Zone; The Outer Limits*

Did You Know?

- American newsman Walter Cronkite coined the term "British Invasion" on a February 7, 1964, edition of his newscast when he stated, "The British Invasion this time goes by the code name Beatlemania."

- The Vince Lombardi Trophy, which is given to the winners of each Super Bowl, is named for legendary Green Bay Packers coach Vince Lombardi, who led the Packers to the victory in the first two Super Bowls. The trophy has been awarded since Super Bowl I.

- Great Britain had its own sci-fi TV craze in the 1960s, but it was a bit different from what was seen in America. British shows, such as *Fireball XL5*, *Thunderbirds*, and *Captain Scarlett and the Mysterons* were huge hits that used puppets instead of live actors. The concept was popular in Britain but was never picked up by networks in the US. The '60s British sci-fi show, *Dr. Who*, did gain an American following, though, after it was syndicated, usually on public television, throughout the US in the late '70s and early '80s.

- Although hippies and bikers could be found in most industrialized countries in the 1960s, Britain had some of its own unique '60s subcultures. The Mods were young people who liked scooters, the rock band The Who, and large military overcoats. The Mods often engaged in brawls with the Rockers, who were basically bikers.

- Gene Roddenberry, the creator of *Star Trek*, once described the original series as a "*Wagon Train* to the stars." The quote was actually emblematic of the '60s, as Rodenberry referenced a hit Western to describe his new sci-fi show.

1960s Science

The Worst Earthquake in History

If you were living in South America on May 22, 1960, or serving in the military in Hawaii, the Philippines, Japan, or Australia, chances are you remember that day well. For those of you who weren't around yet, that was the day when the Valdivia earthquake rocked Chile. The massive quake measured 9.5 on the magnitude scale, leveling buildings throughout the nation, which is essentially a long strip of land in the Andes Mountains.

The worse part, though, was the tsunamis it caused that made landfall all across the Pacific, including hitting Hilo, Hawaii with 35-foot waves.

The final death toll tally for the Valdivia earthquake is still unknown, but it may be as high as 6,000 dead with about $7 billion in 2021 inflation-adjusted damages. The entire Chilean city of Valdivia was leveled, and rural areas were disconnected from Santiago and the other major Chilean cities for several months.

The tremors could be felt throughout South America, and the economic and social tremors from the earthquake and tsunamis lasted throughout the '60s in Chile and the Southern Cone region of South America. Seismologists have said that such a powerful earthquake occurs only once every 50 years or so.

Are we due for another Valdivia magnitude quake?

The Apollo Program

When the Soviets launched the Sputnik satellite, it rocked the world, and when the Soviet cosmonaut (that was the Russian term for astronaut) Yuri Gagarin became the first human in space on April 12, 1961, it caused a bit of a national emergency. Kennedy was already dealing with the Soviets and Cubans on Terra Firma with mixed results, so he knew that the Cold War's next major battleground could very well be in space.

So, President Kennedy led the United States on the greatest scientific quest of not only the 1960s but of the 20th century and some would argue all of human history - the Apollo Program.

Just after Gagarin made his epic journey into orbit, the US government began recruiting the nation's best engineers, computer scientists, biologists, pilots, and other generally smart cookies to beat the Soviets in the space race.

But the Americans weren't just going to go to space; they planned to be the first on the moon!

Although the first Apollo mission, Apollo 1, ended in tragedy on February 21, 1967, killing all three crew members, it didn't deter NASA or America.

For those of you who can remember, the US - and the world for that matter - had some different attitudes at that time. Everyone mourned the loss of the astronauts but quickly got back in the saddle by launching new missions.

It was the Apollo 11 mission that everyone around the world remembers.

On July 20, 1969, as astronaut Michael Collins orbited the Moon in a Saturn V rocket, his crewmates Buzz Aldrin and Neil Armstrong became the first men on the Moon. They planted the American flag and Armstrong stated on live TV, "One small step for man, one giant leap for mankind."

It truly was one of the greatest scientific leaps in human history.

Bulletproof

You've no doubt heard and probably used the term "bulletproof" at some point in your life, although it isn't truly accurate. "Bullet-resistant" probably more accurately describes the material Kevlar, which is used to make vests, helmets, and other materials.

Did you know Kevlar was invented in the 1960s by a Polish American chemist named Stephanie Kwolek?

Kwolek was born in 1923, into a man's world, to say the least. But she studied hard, showed a lot of promise, and was admitted to and graduated from Carnegie Mellon University with a degree in chemistry. She then went to work for DuPont, experimenting with different chemicals before joining a team that worked on developing a lightweight polymer to use in car tires.

After conducting several experiments with different polymers, Kwolek and her team invented the polymer known as poly-paraphenylene terephthalamide (K29) in 1965, which was branded as Kevlar.

Not long after Kevlar was invented, it was used by the troops in Vietnam, but it also has many peaceful uses. Kevlar can be found in car tires, canoes, tennis rackets, and shoes among a plethora of other items we use every day.

Not the Vulcan

During the '60s, sci-fi fans around the world were introduced to the fictional Dr. Spock, but if you followed the news, or had children during the decade, you were also probably familiar with child development expert Dr. Benjamin Spock.

Spock wrote 13 books and countless articles during his long healthcare career, becoming a pioneer in the field of psychology in the process. But the Columbia-educated medical doctor didn't limit his activities to child psychology, he was also an anti-war activist and a genuine celebrity.

Spock's (his name is Dutch, not Vulcan, in case you're wondering!) background was humble enough and his Ivy League medical education was pretty standard for the pre-World War II era, but it was after the war that the good doctor began making a name for himself. In 1946, Spock's first book, *Baby and Childcare*, hit the shelves, forever changing the way childcare was done.

Before Spock, parents were told that they should let their children cry, feed them, and put them to bed at certain times, and place them on their backs when they sleep.

Spock opposed most of these ideas, with some - such as the placement of the babies on their bellies when they sleep - later proving to be a leap forward in medicine. Other ideas, such as putting children on vegan diets, have proved to be less helpful.

No matter what Spock advocated, though, there's no denying that he was one of the most influential medical and scientific minds of the 1960s.

When Free Love Got Easier

Until the last few years, the 1960s was the most tumultuous period in American history. You've seen how politics and culture quickly changed over this ten-year period, and a lot of that had to do with science. Yes, as the often-crazy social currents of the 60s were swirling about, different scientific advances seemed to put an exclamation point on everything that was happening.

We've seen how the Apollo Program brought the world together and how the invention of Kevlar forever changed warfare and law enforcement.

But scientific advances in the 1960s also shifted the very idea of love and sex in the modern world.

It all began when the FDA approved an otherwise little-known pharmaceutical company named Searle to market the world's first oral birth contraceptive to the public in 1960. Although not immediately a big seller, largely because it wasn't legally available in many places, Enovid, the brand name of the first birth control pill, gradually caught on by the end of the decade.

It just so happens that "the pill," as it became to be known, coincided with the era of "free love." Or maybe "the pill" was responsible for it? Either way, it revolutionized modern society in many ways. It gave women more options, allowed millions to work full-time, and is often credited with being the catalyst of the second wave of American feminism.

Have a Heart!

Next to the brain, there isn't an organ in the human body that is as vital to keeping us alive. It's simple: if the heart stops pumping blood, you die! Although ancient people knew of the heart's true importance, there was little to nothing they could do once a person's ticker started going bad.

They could offer some herbal remedies, or pray, which is what they usually did, but when a person's heart truly gave out, there was nothing they could do.

But then medical science advanced so much that, in the 1960s, the first heart transplants took place.

Dr. James Hardy performed the first heart transplant at the University of Mississippi medical center in Jackson, Mississippi on January 24, 1964. As incredible as the feat was itself, it was made even more incredible by the fact that the heart that Dr. Hardy put in his patient, Boyd Rush, was a chimpanzee's. Rush lived for about an hour and a half before dying, but the operation was declared a success.

It was time to try the first human-to-human heart transplant.

South African heart surgeon Christiaan Barnard performed the first human-to-human heart transplant on Louis Washkansky on December 3, 1967, in Cape Town, South Africa. Although Washkansky died 18 days later, Barnard's technique was ruled a success and was duplicated more than 100 times in 1968.

Most of the patients who received heart transplants in the 1960s didn't live longer than a few months, but the advances made are still being felt by heart patients all over the world.

1960s Science Quiz

1. What was the brand name of the first publicly available birth control pill?

2. What was the number of the Apollo mission that landed on the moon?

3. The world's most powerful earthquake happened in what country?

4. In _____ Kevlar was invented.

5. Dr. _____ performed the first human-to-human heart transplant.

6. Dr. Benjamin Spock was known for what field of science?

7. In _____ Soviet cosmonaut Yuri Gagarin became the first human in space.

8. The world's first heart transplant involved putting the heart of what animal into a person?

9. In scientific terms, Kevlar is a _____.

10. Who said: "One small step for man, one giant leap for mankind"?

Answers

1. Enovid
2. 11
3. Chile
4. 1965
5. Christiaan Barnard
6. Child psychology
7. 1961
8. Chimpanzee
9. Polymer
10. Neil Armstrong

Did You Know?

- Although Enovid became the world's first birth control pill, it was initially released in 1957 for the treatment of menstrual problems. Although Canada and the UK are traditionally more socially liberal than the US, the governments of those two countries didn't allow the pill as a birth control prescription until 1961, one year after the US.

- When the crew of Apollo 11 landed on the surface of the Moon, it fulfilled President Kennedy's ten-year pledge to put a man on the Moon. Five more Apollo missions landed astronauts on the Moon. The Soviets began their own project to land cosmonauts on the Moon, but after failures in the late '60s, they gave up on the idea.

- Dr. Spock was an accomplished athlete in his younger years, winning a gold medal with the US rowing team at the 1924 Summer Olympics in Paris, France.

- Since Kevlar was first invented, eight more grades of varying strength have been developed.

- The city of Valdivia, Chile was a center of German immigration in the 1800s, which influenced the city's architecture and cuisine. The earthquake devastated Valdivia's local economy, but by the 1980s, it began to rebound.

CHAPTER 3:

THE 1970S

1970s History

Massacre in Munich

When it was announced that the 1972 Summer Olympics would be held in Munich, West Germany, it was viewed by many as the world coming to terms with the past and present. It was the first time the Olympics would be held in Germany since Hitler and the Nazis hosted the 1936 Summer Games, so the new West German government wanted to show the world the country's new face.

West Germany also wanted to show the communist bloc that the West was the best!

But it all went wrong when a little-known Palestinian militant group named Black September decided to take the Israeli Olympic team hostage on September 5.

Needless to say, it put a damper on West Germany's big chance to change its image.

There's no doubt that if you're a Boomer reading this, you remember these events well. And if you're a post-Boomer, you should know that the 1970s was a decade of terrorism across the industrialized world. Post-New Left radicals in America, such as the Weather Underground, bombed government facilities across the country, while in Europe leftists such as the German Red Army Faction, the Italian Red Brigades, and Irish IRA cooperated with Palestinian groups to bomb targets, commit kidnappings and assassinations, and hijack passenger airliners.

In retrospect, it probably would have been more surprising if something *didn't* happen at the Munich games.

If you remember the Black September attack at the Munich games, then you probably also recall the photo of the terrorists wearing ski masks standing on the balcony of the complex.

The terrorists demanded the release of more than 200 militant Palestinians as well as members of the West German Red Army faction. They also wanted a jet fully fueled and ready to take them to the Middle East.

The West German authorities agreed, but when the militants attempted to board the plane on September 6, they were attacked by West German anti-terrorist commandos. The casualty count was 11 Israelis, five Black September members, and one West German police officer dead. The world was shocked and frightened by the event, but the games continued.

Well, they continued after a 34-hour hiatus.

The Massacre in Munich truly marked the end of an age in innocence in the world. Before that time, all nations, even fascist and communist nations, could compete and rub shoulders in relatively goodwill at the Olympics, but after the 1972 Summer Games, everyone knew that the world had drastically changed.

You no doubt felt it yourself after the Games.

Watergate and President Nixon

As you remember, when Richard Milhous Nixon was elected the thirty-seventh president of the United States of America, it was during a time of turmoil. Nixon ran on a campaign of getting tough with communists and hippies, but also agreeing to some of the demands of the civil rights movement. The people decided to take a chance on Nixon, who was a former vice president, failed gubernatorial candidate of California, and loser of the 1960s presidential election to Kennedy.

Nixon came through on many things, such as ending American involvement in Vietnam, not challenging civil rights legislation, and generally stabilizing the country's social issues. He also "opened up" China by meeting with Mao Zedong and entered arms reduction talks with the Soviets, beginning the period of the Cold War known as the *Détente* or "cooling off."

Nixon also tackled the rising crime rate by initiating a "War on Drugs" and a "get tough on crime" philosophy. It all made Nixon extremely popular, gaining him re-election by a large margin in 1972.

But let's face it, Nixon's best remembered for the Watergate scandal.

Watergate was the name of the Washington, D.C. hotel where the Democrat Party was headquartered in the summer of 1972. Some of Nixon's aides arranged for a group of guys known as the "Plumbers", who were led by G. Gordon Liddy, to break into the offices, steal information, and place wiretaps.

The scandal was brought to light by the *New York Times*, leading the House of Representatives to impeach Nixon. "Tricky Dick," as he became known as, resigned from office on August 9, 1974, before the Senate could convict him.

More scandals followed, as did several criminal convictions. Vice President Gerald Ford, who became president when Nixon resigned, pardoned Nixon, which opened the way for the Democrats to gain seats in the House and Senate and for a peanut farmer from Georgia to win the presidency in 1976.

Celebrating 200 Years of America

Overall, the 1970s was kind of a "ho-hum" decade in a lot of ways. We'll get to that a bit more when we look at the pop culture of the '70s, but overall, it was sort of a transition from the '60s into the '80s.

And the people knew it. At least, they did in the United States. The people were over the '60s; they were tired of the crime and social unrest and ready for something new. The change of the 1980s was still a few years away, but in the meantime, Americans were treated to a celebration of the Declaration of Independence.

Beginning in 1975, celebrations kicked off around America for its Bicentennial. A unique logo was chosen for the celebration and commemorative quarter, half-dollar, and dollar coins were struck at the US mints in Philadelphia and Denver. Commemorative stamps were also printed, which all led up to the big events on July 4, 1976.

You Boomers and a few of you Gen Xers, no doubt remember the July 4 celebrations that year!

The Bicentennial was such an important event in American history that it had a major impact on just about every aspect of society. Bicentennial-themed episodes of sitcoms ranging from *Barney Miller* to *All in the Family* were produced, and the Saturday morning cartoon *Schoolhouse Rock!* aired a series of historical and civic episodes just for the Bicentennial.

If you look around the United States today, or probably even your own home, it won't take you long to find some vestiges of the Bicentennial - maybe some commemorative coins in your drawer, or some other souvenirs from a celebration - chances are you're holding onto something from that momentous occasion!

What Was the Deal with Those Gas Prices?

No doubt another thing you remember about the swinging '70s was long lines at the gas pumps - if there was even gas available - and high prices. A large reason for those problems was the Yom Kippur War in 1973, which was fought by Israel against Egypt, Jordan, and Syria, and the 1979 Islamic Revolution in Iran (we'll get to that a bit later). But to understand all of this, you have to understand the nature of international oil production and OPEC's role in it.

OPEC stands for the Organization of Petroleum Exporting Countries, and as the name states, it comprises some of the largest oil-producing countries in the world. Many of the OPEC nations were and still are in the Middle East and are predominantly Islamic nations, such as Saudi Arabia, Kuwait, and Iraq; although some African nations, including Angola and Nigeria, and the South American nation of Venezuela, are also members. The major oil-producing nations of the United States, Canada, Russia/USSR, Mexico, and Brazil are not and have never been members of OPEC.

Since its formation in 1960, Saudi Arabia was essentially the leading nation of OPEC, which became a political organization in many ways.

When the Yom Kippur War broke out in October 1973, the Saudis thought they'd do their part to help the Arab-Islamic nations by conducting an oil embargo on most Western nations. The Saudis argued that since the United States and many other Western nations funded the Israeli military, it was their only way of fighting back.

The Yom Kippur War ended after just over two weeks as a tactical victory for the Israelis and a political victory for Egypt (Syria didn't come out so well), but the oil embargo was a sticking point in the negotiations. After some negotiating by American Secretary of State Henry Kissinger and OPEC and Israeli diplomats, OPEC oil started flowing again, the gas lines ended, and prices stabilized.

As for the 1979 crisis...keep reading to learn about that!

Drinking the Kool-Aid

Every one of you reading this has no doubt heard and probably used the term "drinking the Kool-Aid." Today, it's usually to refer to a person or people who unquestionably follows a person or idea.

But did you know that the origin of the terms is from one of the most tragic events not only in the history of the 1970s but modern history, for that matter?

On November 18, 1978, American cult leader Jim Jones forced 908 of his followers - men, women, and children - to drink a particularly poisonous mix of potassium cyanide and potassium chloride from a vat of Kool-Aid. This was right after Jones ordered the assassination of California Congressman Leo Ryan, who had just arrived at the cult compound known as "Jonestown" in the isolated backcountry of the South American nation of Guyana.

Within hours, the world learned about the horror in the jungle, but the more that was revealed, the more confusing it all was.

Who were these people?
Why did they willingly commit suicide?
And most importantly, who was Jim Jones?

The people were all members of an obscure cult called the People's Temple, which was led by the charismatic Jim Jones. Jones preached a bizarre theology that mixed elements of Christianity with communism and civil rights era politics. But as strange as it was, he attracted plenty of followers of all racial backgrounds who began to see Jones as God.

He told his followers he *was* God.

As with all cult leaders, Jones had to have complete control over his followers. So, he bought some land in an isolated region of the fairly isolated South American country of Guyana. Jonestown opened in the summer of 1977, but it didn't take long for things to unravel.

The community had problems supporting itself, and even in the jungles of Guyana, Jones lost his grip on his followers. In the end, he made the diabolical decision to force his followers to drink the laced Kool-Aid. Some did it willingly, while others were coerced at gunpoint.

Children who knew something was wrong can be heard crying on audiotapes of the event.

Whether you view the Jonestown Massacre as one of the worst mass suicides or murders in modern history or not, it was one of the biggest historical events of the 1970s and quite a way to end the decade.

But there was still one last world-changing event that took place in the '70s.

Problems in Iran

In the decades after World War II, the UK and the US supported the royal Pahlavi Dynasty in Iran. The ruler was often just referred to in common terms as "the Shah," which is just the Farsi/Iranian name for "king."

Although Iran/Persia has been an Islamic country for centuries, it's always been a bit different from most of its neighbors. Most of the people are ethnically Persian, which varies from the Arabs to their west or the Pakistanis and other people to their east. Persians are also predominantly Shia Muslims, which has often put them at odds with the majority Sunni Islamic world.

This uniqueness put modern Iran in a position where it was often a bridge between East and West, but by the late 1970s, the Pahlavi rulers had grown corrupt, and the people were tired of them.

A revolution broke out in January 1978 that quickly turned religious.

After the Islamists, who were led by Ruhollah Khomeini, took control of the country in February 1979, and proclaimed the Islamic Republic, things got even crazier.

Militant students took control of the American embassy on November 4, 1979, taking more than 60 hostages. The crisis lasted 444 days, with Americans coast to coast tying yellow ribbons on trees, light posts, and even entire buildings as a sign of support and solidarity.

Between the Jonestown Massacre and the hostage crisis, most people were more than happy to be done with the '70s.

1970s History Quiz

1. In what country did the Jonestown Massacre take place?

2. What happened to President Nixon once the Watergate scandal went public?

3. _____ is the name of the organization/cartel of some of the world's leading oil producers and exporters.

4. Most Iranians are ethnically _____ and _____ Muslims.

5. What did Americans celebrate in 1976?

6. Who was the US Congressman that was assassinated by members of Jim Jones's Peoples Temple in 1978?

7. The _____ war set off the 1973 oil embargo.

8. The terrorist group that took the Israeli athletes as hostages during the 1972 Summer Olympics was?

9. The men who carried out dirty work for President Nixon were known as the _____.

10. Where were the 1972 Summer Olympics held?

Answers

1. Guyana

2. He was impeached by the House of Representatives and then resigned from office in 1974.

3. Organization of Petroleum Exporting Countries or OPEC

4. Persian; Shia/Shiite

5. The Bicentennial of the country.

6. Leo Ryan

7. Yom Kippur

8. Black September

9. The Plumbers

10. Munich, West Germany

Did You Know?

- The first location of Jim Jones's Peoples Temple was in Indianapolis, Indiana. Before moving to Guyana, he opened several locations throughout California, and he was seen as a legitimate preacher and activist by many on the left.

- The 1970s was also the era of "Second-wave feminism." Although "bra-burning" in the late '60s is often associated with Second-wave feminism, it became a movement that greatly influenced the mainstream in the '70s. *Roe v. Wade* made abortion legal in the US in 1973 and activists such as Betty Friedan and Gloria Steinem became household names, although not always happily so!

- Black September was so-called because it began its operations in September 1970 during an insurgency against the King Hussein of Jordan.

- Gerald Ford was Richard Nixon's second vice president. Former Maryland Governor Spiro Agnew was Nixon's first vice president, but as the spotlight from the Watergate scandal was beamed onto the White House, Agnew's fraudulent business activities while he was governor came to light. He resigned from the vice presidency in 1973 and pleaded no contest to a felony charge of tax evasion.

- Numismatists have generally enjoyed collecting Bicentennial commemorative coins and proof sets, although many find the design on the Eisenhower dollar a bit strange. The obverse side depicts his bust in profile, as with all the other years of the coin, but the reverse side is of the Liberty Bell imposed over the Moon. Many find the historical relevance and the physical design of the reverse side out of place.

1970s Pop Culture

Did You Keep Your 8-track Tapes?

I know some of you Boomers remember with fondness rolling down the street in your Camaro - or maybe it was a Nova - with your windows rolled down, the wind blowing through your long hair, and Foghat blasting on your 8-track deck.

"Slow ride...take it."

Then the sound of a "click." And the song resumes!

Yes, the 8-track tape was one of those crazy '70s things - actually, they first hit the market in the mid '60s - that can only be found today on eBay and possibly flea markets.

You're probably wondering why 8-tracks cut out in the middle of songs like they did. Well, 8-tracks were tapes, but to put them into portable cases, the tracks had to be divided into four pairs. And since most musicians at the time didn't make albums specifically for 8-tracks, to fit all the songs of an album onto a tape, often songs had to be spliced between tracks.

Of course, that was just the main problem with 8-tracks.

They were also big and bulky, which meant that only so many could fit into a car. Thankfully, cars of the '70s were also big. Thankfully, by the end of the '70s, cassette technology had advanced to the point that tapes were compact and didn't jump in the middle of songs.

8-tracks were a thing of the past by the late '80s, and most people had forgotten about them. But if you still have your tapes or player, you could get a nice price from a collector.

The Gold Age of Sitcoms

The 1940s and '50s may have been the Golden Age of Television, but when it comes to sitcoms specifically, no decade can beat the 1970s. As we've already seen with *The Honeymooners*, sitcoms weren't necessarily new in the 1970s, but they certainly weren't as prominent on TV before that time. Hour-long dramas were the most common and popular style of programming, but by the early '70s, TV tastes had changed.

People were on the go a lot more - with jobs, families, and hobbies, so sitting around for an hour was losing its luster—remember, this is before VCRs, never mind TiVo, DVR, or streaming services.

So, network executives flooded the airwaves with a host of new half-hour comedies. A number of them had not-so-subtle social messages, such as the Norman Lear produced shows *Good Times*, *All in the Family*, and *One Day at a Time*, among others. Other programs, like *Happy Days*, were more mundane, while some were just silly — do you remember *Three's Company*?

And then there were a whole host of shows you've probably forgotten about or would like to forget. With there being so many sitcoms made in the '70s, there were certainly a few clunkers like *The Ropers* and *Flying High*.

Keep on Truckin'

If you were a teen or older in the 1970s, chances are you heard and used the phrase "Keep on Truckin'" at some point. What did it mean? Well, you could say that it epitomized the decade in many ways because for most people, it was simply a way of saying "it's cool, man" and "take it easy." The term became so widespread that it could be found on stickers, usually accompanied by an image of a man striding with his left foot far in front of his body. By the end of the '70s, you could find many different versions of the striding man on t-shirts, hats, and stickers.

So how did this pre-internet meme begin?

In 1968, cartoonist Robert Crumb penned the slogan and striding man in the first issue of *Zap Comix*, which was a periodical popular with the hippie set. As the slogan and depiction grew into a legitimate meme in the hippie and counter-culture circles in the early 1970s, it made its way into the mainstream by the mid-70s.

By 1976, nearly everyone had heard the phrase "Keep on Truckin'" or had used it themselves. In fact, it was so common that it was even said on episodes of the sitcoms *Sandford and Son* and *Maude*.

So, remember, the next time you get bummed out or let down, just channel your inner '70s spirit, man, and "Keep on Truckin'"!

Do a Little Dance

You can't talk about '70s pop culture without at least mentioning disco, right? It seemed like it was everywhere, from the blockbuster film *Saturday Night Fever* to Top 40 hits such as Gloria Gaynor's "I Will Survive" to Van McCoy's "The Hustle," and of course KC and the Sunshine Band's "Get Down Tonight."

Even rockers like Kiss came out with a disco-influenced album, *Dynasty*, in 1979.

But how big was disco?

Disco music was big for a few years, but the genre was pretty much over by 1981 — most Americans continued to prefer classic rock and even those who gravitated towards "alternative" musical styles chose punk, new wave, and metal over disco.

Although disco did make a bit of a splash in other English-speaking countries and Western Europe, its worldwide reach was minimal.

And though A-list movie stars such as Sylvester Stallone, Faye Dunaway, and Al Pacino all partied at the famous disco club, Studio 54 in New York City, most Americans would have never been allowed inside its doors.

Disco had long-term influences on American culture and music, but its immediate impact was fairly short-term. By 1980, most Americans were tired of disco and the phrase "disco's dead" became just as popular in 1979 as "Keep on Truckin'" was in '75.

Still, you have to admit there were some catchy disco tunes, and it's fun to watch old footage of people getting down on the dancefloor.

Star Wars

A long time ago in a galaxy far away…And with those nine words, a global phenomenon was born in 1977 that continues to this day. In case you've lived in isolation for the last 45 years, those are the first words in the hit film *Star Wars*, which spawned two successful sequels, three prequels, later sequels, cartoons, one best-forgotten holiday special, billions of dollars in merchandise, and legions of loyal fans whose numbers seemingly grow every day.

And it all began with writer and director George Lucas' idea of making a Flash Gordon feature film.

When Lucas couldn't get the rights to Flash Gordon, he decided to go his own way and create a unique space epic. Unique is putting it mildly.

With an $11 million budget, which was quite large for the time, Lucas was able to use state-of-the-art special effects and film in exotic locations, but he did have to save a bit on actors. He did get film veteran James Earl Jones to do the voice of Darth Vader, British screen legend Peter Cushing had a small role, and his fellow British legend, Alec Guinness, had a larger role, but most of the main actors were relative unknowns.

Star Wars carved out a career for Harrison Ford, who played Han Solo, but not so much for Mark Hamill, who was Luke Skywalker, and Carrie Fisher, who played Skywalker's sister, Princess Leia.

The movie's unique formula proved to be a box office, critical, and cultural success.

Audiences were awed by the special effects and plot that mixed elements of sci-fi with Westerns. The new, fresh faces actually helped the film, and going to see *Star Wars* soon became the cool thing to do.

Then came the merchandising!

Movies before *Star Wars* had accompanying merchandise campaigns, but *Star Wars* brought things to a whole new level, as a whole line of toys were aimed at the children of older Baby Boomers and the Silent Generation. Most of the toys were marketed for boys, with a complete action figure line (which was a relatively new concept), numerous playsets for the action figures, toy guns and "light sabers," costumes, books, stickers, and just about anything else you can think of.

The success of the movie itself, combined with the merchandising campaign, left the people wanting more of the *Star Wars* franchise. They'd get their wish, of course, but they'd have to wait for the 1980s.

Really - a Pet Rock?

There's no doubt that the culture of the 1970s was a little off the wall at times. You can't really blame the people of the decade, though, as they were coming out of the turbulent 60s and about to enter the manic 80s, so it was bound to be a quirky decade that had traits of what came before and after it. But there's one '70s pop culture phenomenon that seems to defy all logic...the pet rock.

Yes, the pet rock really was a thing.

The idea came about when a guy named Gary Dahl was having a few beers with some friends in a Los Gatos, California bar. He noticed that the conversations often veered to pets, particularly many of the problems associated with pets.

So, Dahl came up with the bright idea to sell rocks and market them as pets.

As dumb as the idea sounds, it made Dahl a millionaire and a bit of a cultural icon. Each approximately two-inch rock came packed in straw in a little cardboard box, but what made the item so popular was the 32-page booklet, *The Care and Training of Your Pet Rock,* that was included with each rock.

The booklet gave instructions on how to care for the rocks in a matter-of-fact dry style of humor that came naturally to Dahl. Packed within the instructions were plenty of jokes and puns. One of my favorite instruction reads:

> "If you are getting blood out of your rock, you should contact the Internal Revenue Service immediately. They've been attempting to do this very thing for years."

The pet rock has attempted to make a comeback, but it remains to be seen if a new generation will find the humor in something that's clearly "so '70s."

1970s Pop Culture Quiz

1. What year did the blockbuster film *Star Wars* hit the theaters?

2. The Keep On Truckin' cartoon/meme was first written by _____.

3. What was the name of the New York City disco club that became world-famous in the '70s?

4. _____ was the "inventor" of the pet rock.

5. What old sci-fi character inspired George Lucas to write *Star Wars*?

6. This television producer created many "socially conscious" sitcoms in the 1970s.

7. One of the problems with 8-track tapes was that they _____.

8. What band performed the hit disco tune "Get Down Tonight"?

9. _____ was one of the veteran British actors who had a role in *Star Wars*.

10. What was *Star Wars'* budget?

Answers

1. 1977

2. Robert Crumb

3. Studio 54

4. Gary Dahl

5. Flash Gordon

6. Norman Lear

7. They were too big and bulky; the tracks would change in the middle of songs

8. KC and the Sunshine Band

9. Peter Cushing; Alec Guinness

10. $11 million

Did You Know?

- 8-tracks were primarily popular in the English-speaking world, although they did catch on a bit in West Germany and Italy. Since the 8-track era was so short, being done by the early '80s, most countries easily bypassed the technology and went straight from LPs to cassette tapes.

- Many people point to July 12, 1979, as an important date in the death of disco. On that date, the Chicago White Sox baseball team did a promotion at Comiskey Park, where fans could bring a disco album and get admitted for the low price of $.98. The fans then burned the albums in the middle of the field, but things got out of hand, and it turned into a riot. After that, it seemed to most people that disco was truly dead.

- *Star Wars'* budget was modest but not minuscule for the 1970s. What was impressive, though, was how much the film made. It made a whopping $775.8 million at the box office, making it one of the most successful films of all time in terms of net profits and profits adjusted for inflation.

- The 1970s gave birth to the term "jiggle TV." As you can guess from the term, it referred to TV shows that used a lot of sex appeal, and plenty of tight shirts, exposed midriffs, cleavage, and tight pants, to attract viewers. In addition to *Three's Company*, *Charlie's Angels* and *Wonder Woman* are considered examples of jiggle TV.

- Perhaps connected to Keep on Truckin', the 1970s also experienced a trucking craze. Ordinary people began buying and using CBs and trucking themed shows and movies were popular, including the shows *Movin' On* and *B.J. and the Bear* and the 1978 film *Convoy*.

1970s Science

America's Railway

Americans are often teased, usually by Europeans, about their reliance on cars for transportation, especially gas-guzzling trucks, and SUVs. Europeans like to lecture about the virtues of public transportation and how the European rail system is so effective and efficient.

Well, effective yes, but efficient…we'll leave that for another time.

The reality is that the United States is much larger and less densely populated than Europe, making providing all Americans with rail more difficult. But it's also true that the US was primarily a rail nation until the 1960s.

After World War II, a few things happened in the US that pushed Americans away from the railways and toward automobiles. First, cars became more affordable, and the economy was doing well, so more and more Americans could own cars. Second, the construction of the Interstate Highway System (remember that?) connected the country in a way that made automobile travel quicker, easier, and safer.

But by the late 1960s, as rail travel declined, there were calls to salvage what was left of America's passenger rails. The Rail Passenger Service Act of 1970 essentially gave money to the struggling passenger lines of America, which were almost entirely consolidated on May 1, 1971, when the private rail company Amtrak went into service.

Amtrak was/is technically a private corporation, but it has depended on government subsidies from the beginning, which has made it the target of criticism.

In terms of technology, Amtrak offered nothing new in terms of its engines, but its quick transformation of a collage of private lines that crisscrossed the nation was nothing short of phenomenal. Amtrak immediately cut the number of passenger routes from 366 to 184 and used 1,200 of the available 3,000 passenger cars at the time.

Amtrak never proved to be the revolutionary change to American transportation that some promised, nor was it the failure others said it would be. Americans slowly began riding the Amtrak rails more and more in the '70s, proving that although it may never overtake automobile or air travel, there will always be a place for passenger rail travel in the US.

The Emergence of Color TV

When TV advanced from black-and-white to color, it was a bit like the recent transition from standard to high-definition TV. The major difference, though, was that the transition from standard to high-def took place relatively quickly, while the transition from black-and-white to color was a longer process.

Without getting too much into all the technical terms, the first television sets displayed images in shades of gray known as grayscale. The idea of color television was around as early as the '40s and some American TV stations even began showing some programs in color in the '50s, but the problem was that most people still saw those shows in black and white.

Color TVs were rare and awfully expensive throughout the 1960s.

To demonstrate this, in 1964 only 3% of households in the US had color TV sets. The majority of network programming was still in black-and-white, and color TV sets were still expensive at that time, but by the late 1960s things quickly changed.

As the 1970s rolled in, the combination of lower color TV prices and all major networks broadcasting in color, along with all new shows being done in color, meant that in 1972 more than 50% of American households had color TV sets.

Millions of American children could finally watch their favorite Saturday morning cartoons in full color.

Working Together

On July 17, 1975, millions of people around the world watched in anticipation as the three American astronauts—Thomas Stafford, Vance Brand, and Deke Slayton—docked their Saturn rocket with a Soviet Soyuz capsule manned by cosmonauts Alexei Neonov and Valeri Kubasov. The two crews conducted joint experiments for just under 48 hours before saying "Goodbye" and "Dasvidanyia" and then returning to their respective countries back on Earth.

The mission became known as the Apollo-Soyuz mission, and as important as it may have been geopolitically and historically, it also had some important scientific implications.

The Apollo-Soyuz mission opened the way for future international space missions and also showed scientists how it was possible to connect two quite different capsules. The Soviets, and later the Russians, in particular, benefited from the Apollo-Soyuz mission by taking the knowledge that they gained from it to build the Mir Space Station in 1986. The Mir was the first space station assembled in orbit, and it was only possible due to some of the techniques and technologies used during the Apollo-Soyuz mission.

The Mir later opened the door for the construction of the current International Space Station now in orbit.

All of this was only possible, though, because Cold War tensions chilled out a bit in the '70s.

It Seemed Like a Good Idea at the Time

Transportation technology was kind of the theme of 1970s science. There was the introduction of Amtrak in America, then the Apollo-Soyuz mission, but probably the coolest scientific innovation of the '70s was the commercialization of the Concorde jet.

If you're forty-five or older, it's pretty hard to forget the Concorde. The Concorde was the first of its kind supersonic jet that could get up to speeds of Mach 2.02 or 1,330 mph - now that's fast!

The Concorde was first built in 1968, but the British and French governments signed a treaty shortly after to jointly develop the jet for commercial use. The plan was for the British-French consortium to sell the jets to various airline companies, but British Airways and Air France were the only two companies to ever operate the jet exclusively.

The first flight of the Concorde took January 21, 1976, and for a time it seemed like it was going to be the wave of the future for international travel. After initial resistance in the US over potential noise created by the Concorde reaching supersonic speed, flights from New York and Washington to London and Paris began in late 1977.

Other destinations to and from major cities around the world followed, and the speed of the Concorde seemed to make it destined to be a success. It only took three and a half hours to fly from New York to Paris, which was less than half the time it took in a subsonic flight.

But with everything else in life, it always comes down to cost.

The price for a seat on a Concorde flight from New York to London ran about $8,000, which was too much for most people. Even rich people often found it difficult to justify doling out that kind of money to make it to their destination a few hours earlier.

Interest in the Concorde eventually fizzled due to high ticket prices, the 9-11 attacks, and the novelty of the technology had worn off, resulting in the jet being decommissioned by British Airways and Air France in 2003. No one can deny that the Concorde had a good run and that it was a major part of 1970s science and technology.

The Birth of Apple

There's a good chance that as you're reading this, you're stopping from time to time to check text messages on your iPhone. Or maybe you're reading this on your iPhone. Or maybe you're getting ready to check your emails on your Mac after you get done reading this.

Whatever the case, there's no doubt that Apple has played a major role not just in modern technology but in popular culture as well. Apple products are everywhere, and as you know, they have a very loyal following. The company has recently moved into other media ventures, launching its own streaming service.

And it all began on April 1, 1976, in the sleepy suburb of Los Altos, California.

It was on that date that Apple founders Steve Jobs, Steve Wozniak, and Ronald Wayne founded their company to sell their home computer, the Apple I.

The Apple I looked and functioned nothing like the Macs of today—it was just the motherboard, keyboard and monitor not included! But it was a revolutionary step forward in consumer electronics and it was successful, so the company incorporated in January 1977. By the end of the decade, the Apple computer sold in stores looked much more like what you see today, leading to the first wave of home computers.

The creation of Apple also led to Silicon Valley becoming what it is today.

The End of Smallpox

Viruses have been around as long as humans have existed, but it was only in the late 1800s that people began to understand that many diseases are spread through germs. "Germ theory," as it's called, was first articulated by Louis Pasteur (1822-1895) in the late 1800s by isolating different biological materials and observing how the germs form in different settings.

There are several different subclassifications of germs. Bacteria is one of the most common forms of germs, but viruses are also a type of germ.

The smallpox virus was a particularly nasty virus that caused painful skin lesions, fever, and death in 35% of all cases. The virus caused millions of deaths throughout history, so when the last naturally occurring case was reported in 1977, it was considered one of the greatest medical advances of the '70s and human history.

Smallpox was eventually defeated through a combination of efforts. The vaccine was developed by Englishman Edward Jenner (1749-1823) in the late 1700s, about 100 years before germ theory, by exposing people to the related but far less lethal cowpox. Through a combination of vaccination, quarantining, and herd immunity, smallpox was eliminated by the mid-1970s in pretty much every country on the planet except the isolated locations of Ethiopia and Somalia.

The last known naturally occurring case of smallpox was in Somalia in 1977, giving the world a bit of relief and allowing scientists to focus their efforts on other deadly diseases.

1970s Science Quiz

1. _____ was one of the two Soviet cosmonauts who took part in the Apollo-Soyuz mission.

2. How fast could the Concorde jets fly?

3. What year did Amtrak begin service?

4. By 1972, _____% of American homes had color TVs.

5. What year was smallpox eradicated?

6. The first Apple computer available on the market was the _____.

7. Amtrak immediately cut the number of passenger train routes from _____ to _____.

8. In what country was the last reported naturally occurring case of smallpox?

9. Steve Jobs, Steve Wozniak, and_____ were the founders of Apple.

10. The Apollo-Soyuz mission allowed the Soviets/Russians to build the _____.

Answers

1. Alexei Neonov; Valeri Kubasov
2. Mach 2.02 or 1,330 mph
3. 1971
4. 50%
5. 1977
6. Apple I
7. 366 to 184
8. Somalia
9. Ronald Wayne
10. Mir Space Station

Did You Know?

- Ronald Wayne is often overlooked as one of the founders of Apple because he only held a 10% share in the original partnership and then sold that for a paltry $800! To make matters worse, he accepted a $1,500 check a year later to forgo any potential claims on the Apple name or intellectual property. To top it all off, in the 1990s, he sold the original paper contract of the deal he had with the other two for $500, which was later sold at an auction for $1.6 million!

- Although Amtrak has most of its lines in the northeast and is most popular there and in Illinois and California, it has stops in 46 of the 48 continental states. There are no Amtrak stops in South Dakota or Wyoming.

- The Russians still use Soyuz craft on their space missions.

- In addition to about half of all American homes having color TVs in 1972, that was also the year that color TVs first outsold black-and-white sets.

- There were 20 Concorde jets built in total, but only 14 were used commercially.

CHAPTER 4:

THE 1980S

1980s History

The Iron Lady

The 1980s was full of larger-than-life personalities who were often given nicknames as colorful as their lives. You had "Ronnie" running the US and "Gorby" was the bigshot in the USSR, while in the UK it was the "Iron Lady" Margaret Thatcher. Thatcher presented herself as a prim and proper Englishwoman, always dressed well, polite, and pleasant, but underneath that polished exterior was a tough as nails woman who was every bit as tough as the men who were the major Cold War power players of the day.

Margaret was born in 1925 and almost immediately in her childhood, she stood out from the other kids. Bright and independent, the future Mrs. Thatcher excelled in academics and decided to go to college when most women couldn't. Then she decided to become a lawyer when most lawyers were overwhelmingly men, and later to enter the overwhelmingly male-dominated "boys club" of politics.

And perhaps even more challenging, she joined the more traditional Conservative Party.

But Thatcher seemed to thrive on the challenges, rising to her party's leadership in the 1970s due to a combination of her sharp intellect, excellent speaking skills, and fresh ideas. Her uncompromising anti-communist stances earned her the nickname the "Iron Lady" from a Soviet journalist in 1976.

Although the nickname was meant as an insult, Thatcher wore it as a badge of honor on her way to becoming the prime minister in 1979.

Thatcher's domestic policies, which became known as "Thatcherism," defined Britain in the 1980s, and her support of the US and Ronald Reagan is cited by many historians as one of the reasons why the West won the Cold War.

Those Were Some Close Calls in '83

The Cuban Missile Crisis may have been the single instance where the Soviet Union and the United States were closest to war, but 1983 was probably the longest stretch that had the most of those close calls.

It all began when Ronald Reagan became president in 1981. He ran on an aggressive anti-communism platform, and combined with Thatcher running the show in Britain, he had the support at home and abroad to carry out a more confrontational Cold War policy. And in March 1983, Reagan didn't hide what he thought about the Soviet Union, calling it an "evil empire" in a speech he delivered to evangelical Christians in Florida.

Needless to say, the Soviets weren't amused.

Then on September 1, 1983, tragedy struck when the Soviets shot down a civilian Korean Air Lines flight that had wandered into their airspace. All 269 people on the plane were killed, including US Congressman Larry McDonald.

The shootdown upped the tension between the East and West, which then nearly boiled over due to another "mistake" on September 26, 1983. On that day, the Soviet early warning system detected an incoming ICBM attack from the US. Thankfully,

Soviet lieutenant colonel Stanislav Petrov thought something wasn't right, especially since the early warning system only showed one American missile headed toward the USSR. Instead of following protocol and reporting the missile through the chain of command, which probably would have set off World War III, Petrov did nothing and saved us all.

At this point, things could've blown up, literally, at any moment, and most people in the world had no idea!

Finally, in November 1983, the NATO forces were conducting combined "war games" exercises in Western Europe that they codenamed "Operation Able Archer."

When Able Archer began on November 7, Soviet intelligence and military officials thought it was a cover for a NATO attack on Eastern Europe, so Warsaw Pact forces went on high alert and were ready to carry out a preemptive attack on Western Europe.

When the NATO forces ended Able Archer on November 11, the Soviets were able to confirm that it was a war game, and everyone could breathe a sigh of relief. Cold War tensions continued through the 1980s, but they were never as high as they were during those months in '83.

The Man with the Aviator Sunglasses

It seems like every decade has its boogeyman. In the 2000s it was Osama Bin Laden, in the '60s it was Castro, in the '70s it was Yasser Arafat, and in the '80s, at least in the US, it was Muamar Gaddafi. Looking back, he was probably crazier than he was dangerous, but he did manage to get under Ronald Reagan's skin.

Gaddafi was part of a military coup that overthrew the king of Libya in 1969, becoming its dictator until he was forcibly removed and killed in 2011.

Before that, though, Gaddafi made quite the impression on geopolitics, as he mixed Arab nationalism with socialism and a little bit of Islamism to create the Libyan Arab Republic. He cozied up to the communist bloc, allowed leftist terrorist groups to train in the desserts of his country, and liked to wear traditional Bedouin robes.

And he also liked to wear military uniforms with aviator sunglasses. But of course, every good dictator wears aviator sunglasses!

What got Gaddafi into trouble with Reagan, though, came when terrorists bombed a West Berlin nightclub popular with US servicemen on April 5,

1986, killing two American soldiers and a Turkish civilian.

The bombing was linked to Libyan intelligence officers, so Reagan responded by ordering aerial bombings of Tripoli and Benghazi, Libya on April 15. Gaddafi didn't go away after the airstrikes, though. He continued to support terrorist groups and just wouldn't go away, but by the end of the decade, he was more of a caricature than a legitimate threat.

As other major events happened around the world in the 1980s, people pretty much forgot about Gaddafi, no matter how hard he tried to stay relevant.

The Challenger Disaster

Every generation can point to one pivotal moment in their lives when something of such historical magnitude happened that they remember exactly what they were doing when they heard the news. It's the phenomenon of "What were you doing when 'X' happened?"

For many of you Boomers reading this, your first "What were you doing?" moment may have been when you learned President Kennedy had been assassinated. For many of your children, their first "What were you doing?" moment took place on

January 28, 1986, when the Space Shuttle Challenger blew up just after takeoff, killing all seven of its crew.

Many kids at the time were watching the flight in school. This was largely because schoolteacher Christa McAuliffe had won a contest to put the first civilian in space. Needless, to say, it was a bit of a traumatic event for those who saw the event in real-time.

It was later determined that the O-rings on the shuttle failed, but as it happened, no one knew what was going on and what we were seeing. Was it sabotage? Was it even real?

Of course, it was very real, and you probably remember that people everywhere were hurt, confused, and scared by the event. Although the country pulled together and rose above the tragedy, it did set NASA back several years.

The Big Crash

In terms of economics, the 1980s is often remembered as a time of economic stability and plenty, where the stock market functioned as a virtual cornucopia of money to fuel the "decade of decadence" and excess. Chances are, some of you reading this made some big bucks back in the '80s, and if so, then you probably also remember the big Wall Street crash known as "Black Monday."

Black Monday happened on October 19, 1987, when 23 of the world's largest stock markets declined drastically, with the Dow Jones Industrial Average (DJIA) dropping 508 and losing 22.6% of its volume that day.

Several factors contributed to the worldwide crash, and despite fears of it turning into something worse, the markets quickly rebounded. Day traders lost a bundle, but if you had a 401K or other long-term stock investments, chances are you ended up alright. Two years later, the DJIA had recovered all of its losses, so most people really didn't notice much of an impact in their portfolios.

The Big Crash of '87 was something that could have been really bad, but the economic momentum of the '80s was just too strong to be held back.

"Tear Down This Wall"

As a Baby Boomer in the West, especially in the US, your life was characterized by the Cold War in many ways. There was always a fear that the missiles could start flying at any moment and your day-to-day life often involved an "us versus them" type mentality.

By the late '80s, that was quickly coming to an end.

This is not to say that the 1980s wasn't still part of the Cold War. We saw the close calls in 1983, and there were also proxy wars between the Soviet Union and the United States in Afghanistan and Central America. However, by the late '80s, it was clear to everyone that the Soviet system was on its last legs.

The USSR's leader, Mikhail Gorbachev, tried to save the Soviet system through reform measures known as *Glasnost* and *Perestroika*, but they only seemed to speed up the system's demise.

Then, sensing that the communist system was coming to an end, President Reagan gave a historic speech in front of the Brandenburg Gate in West, Berlin, West Germany on June 12, 1987. The gate was a historic monument in German history, but when the Cold War began and Germany was divided, it had become part of the Berlin Wall that separated the city and the country. On that day, Reagan said in his speech:

"General Secretary Gorbachev, if you seek peace, if you seek prosperity for the Soviet Union and Eastern Europe, if you seek liberalization, come here to this gate. Mr. Gorbachev, open this gate. Mr. Gorbachev...Mr. Gorbachev, tear down this wall!"

Two years later, on November 9, 1989, the Wall did come down, signaling the end of the Cold War, the end of the '80s, and the beginning of a new era in history.

And just think about it, you were alive to see it all happen...how cool is that?!

1980s History Quiz

1. Operation Able Archer was the codename of _____ that took place in 1983.

2. _____ was the teacher who died in the *Challenger* disaster.

3. What year did the Berlin Wall come tumbling down?

4. Margaret Thatcher was a member of what British political party?

5. Muamar Gaddafi was the dictator of what Middle Eastern country?

6. Mikhail Gorbachev initiated reforms meant to _____ the Soviet Union.

7. The passenger jet the Soviets shot down in 1983 was from what company?

8. How many points did the Dow Jones Industrial Index lose on "Black Monday"?

9. What caused the *Challenger* disaster?

10. President Reagan ordered the _____ of Libya after a terrorist attack in West Berlin.

Answers

1. NATO wargames

2. Christa McAuliffe

3. 1989

4. Conservative

5. Libya

6. Save

7. Korean Airlines/Korean Air

8. 508

9. O-ring failure

10. Aerial bombing

Did You Know?

- Gaddafi was an eccentric guy, to say the least. Even after he became the dictator of his country, he never promoted himself to general and was still often referred to as "The Colonel." He was also known for his entourage of female bodyguards called the "Revolutionary Nuns." He said he chose women because a Muslim assassin would hesitate to kill women.

- If you were wheeling and dealing in the stock market in the '80s, chances are you were referred to as a Yuppie. The term was short for "young upwardly-mobile professional."

- *Glasnost* referred to the idea of "opening," which in the Cold War meant that the Soviet Union allowed more people to visit their country and also permitted more of their people to leave, among other things. *Perestroika* referred to the "restructuring" of the Soviet government and society, allowing for more political dissent and free-market trade.

- As the US and USSR almost came to blows in 1983, the movie *The Day After* was shown on American television on November 20, 1983. It was about nuclear war between the two countries and how it affected people in the American Midwest. *The Day After* was the highest-rated TV movie in history until 2009.

- From April 2 to June 1982, Argentina and Britain fought each other in the Falklands War over the otherwise inconsequential Falklands Islands off the coast of Argentina. Both countries were important allies in Reagan's war against communism, but in the end, the US government sided more with Britain, who won the war.

1980s Pop Culture

From New Wave to Metal

If you're a later Boomer, then you probably have fond memories of rocking out to some of the new musical styles that came out in the '80s. There was the new wave style made popular by groups such as Blondie and the Talking Heads. Or maybe you liked the emerging hair metal bands like Motley Crüe or the Scorpions.

Or if you were really hard, you blasted Slayer on your stereo.

Maybe you got into the early rap/hip hop scene that came out in the '80s with rappers like Kool Moe Dee, Biz Markie, and Fab Five Freddy.

Whatever you were into, there was definitely a musical taste for you in the '80s.

If you're an early Boomer, well, you probably didn't care much for the music, and you probably heard enough of it when your kids were blasting it on their portable cassette players known as "boom boxes" or "ghetto blasters."

And then there was MTV.

As soon as the Music Television Network (all the kids just knew it as MTV) came on the air on August 1, 1981, it changed the way music was consumed and set the tone for the decade. Most of the hip fashions of the '80s - that we'll get to in a bit - became popular through MTV, as did words like "radical," "awesome," and "grody."

Your Kids Couldn't Get Enough Atari

Or maybe *you* couldn't!

The Atari 2600 home console game system was in many homes in the early '80s and was often the source of conflicts over the use of the television.

If you had kids in that decade, you no doubt cringed when your kids wanted to "play Atari" on the main TV in the family room. If you're a bit younger and wondering - yes, most middle-class American homes in the '80s had a primary TV set in the family room/den, while the kitchen often had a smaller set. Mom and Dad also possibly had a set in their bedroom, but the set with the Atari 2600 was in the family room.

The Atari 2600 first came out in 1977, and it was a first-of-its-kind video game console with separate cartridges for the games. In 1979, Mattel launched a video game console called Intellivision, so by the early '80s, the two companies were locked in competition for the gamers of America, and the world!

The graphics on the games paled in comparison to those today, but no one knew any better at the time. Games went for about $50 *back then*, so you can imagine the type of money the nerds were making by creating these games.

In 1983, the American video game console industry was raking in $3.2 billion, but then it all crashed that year.

There were just too many games on the market, and home computers also became less expensive. In 1985, the video game industry dropped to a low of $100 million in revenue, but by the end of the decade, it rebounded when Sega and Nintendo started producing much more advanced consoles with way better graphics.

The Original King of Late Night

Today, it seems that network television late-night talk show hosts are a dime a dozen, but in decades past, they were few and far between. One stood out among all of them - Johnny Carson.

From 1962 to 1992, Johnny Carson ruled the airwaves of late-night television in the US with his NBC show *The Tonight Show Starring Johnny Carson*, but it was during the '80s that Carson was in his prime.

Along with his sidekick Ed McMahon, Carson was a part of millions of American homes by the 1980s. He also helped launch the careers of many comedians, actors, and musicians during that decade.

Fellow 1980s late-night talk show host David Letterman guest-hosted the show several times before scoring his own slot right after Carson, and if you ever watch old episodes on Me TV or YouTube, you may catch Roseanne Barr performing on the show in '85, Jim Carrey doing a set in '83, and Eddie Murphey gracing Carson's stage with a fairly toned-down version of his blue humor in '82.

There's no doubt about it, anyone who was anyone in the entertainment world had to be on Carson in the '80s. It was where the rest of us found out about new movie releases, TV shows, and albums.

In the era before the internet or even celebrity gossip channels, *The Tonight Show with Johnny Carson* was *the* clearinghouse of pop culture news.

After School Specials

One of the most memorable TV trends of the '80s was the ubiquitous nature of what was generally known as "after school specials." These were original, live-action television shows produced by the networks for pre-teens and teens. Due to the nature of the audience, they were generally shown in the afternoon hours, before primetime. Most of these shows were anthologies, with different actors each episode, and were shown on a semi-regular basis, such as once a month.

After school specials actually began in 1973 on the ABC network with the *ABC Afterschool Special*, but by the '80s, both CBS and NBC had versions of the format.

These shows often dealt with topics that affect teens, especially those that were more common at the time. Divorce, drug and alcohol use, child abuse, suicide, rape, and gang violence were just some of the topics dealt with in after school specials.

In retrospect, some of the problems featured in the after-school specials seem trivial by today's standards, and the acting seems stilted and forced, but a number of A-listers got their starts on the *ABC Afterschool Special* in the '80s.

Ben Affleck, Rob Lowe, and Justine Bateman had some of their earliest acting gigs on the *ABC Afterschool Special* in the '80s, so the acting couldn't have been too bad, right?

Big Hair, Acid Washed Jeans, and Hi-top Sneakers

When you think back on the fashion of the '80s, it's really hard to categorize or put it all into one word. Or even a few words. I guess you could say that '80s fashion was "anything goes!"

Sure, there were a few trends that seemed to have lasted the whole decade. Big hair with plenty of mousse or hair spray (people cared less about the ozone layer back then) was the norm, and stone-washed/acid-washed jeans were worn by most people.

Levi was the popular brand, but if you were really cool, you wore Guess.

But other than that, fashion was sort of a hodgepodge of different subcultures. Punk, new wave, metal, country, and hip hop all influenced everyday fashion, and as diverse as those musical styles were, so too were the clothes.

The kids liked to wear pants with a lot of zippers, known as parachute pants, just like Michael Jackson. And they also like to wear hi-top sneakers with their laces undone.

Perhaps influenced by Chuck Norris movies that were coming out every week, it seemed, or any other ninja movie of the time, young men liked to wear muscle shirts emblazoned with Asian script few could read.

Come on guys, I know a few of you reading this had one of those shirts. And you probably also had a matching headband you'd put on when you practiced with your 'nunchucks' in the backyard!

Ladies, you probably had at least one jacket with shoulder pads to make your shoulders look bigger...well, I honestly can't think of any reason people thought that was cool.

And then there was the cooler-than-cool look of wearing a t-shirt, pants, and a dress jacket, in pastel colors, of course.

Miami Vice

If there was one TV show that encapsulated the '80s, it was *Miami Vice*. From 1984 through 1990, millions of Americans tuned to NBC every Friday night to watch the latest adventures of detectives Sonny Crocket, played by Don John, and Ricardo Tubbs, acted by Philip Michael Thomas.

The show was an immediate hit, as it brought together everything that people loved about the '80s: cool music, cutting-edge clothing styles, fast cars, violence, beautiful women in bikinis, handsome cops making arrests, and of course, plenty of cocaine.

Miami Vice may have reflected many of the pop culture styles of the '80s, but it was also a great influencer. The t-shirt and suit look mentioned earlier and the emphasis on pastel colors was the result of *Miami Vice*'s popularity. Before Crocket and Tubbs hit the small screen, no one in the US would have thought to dress like them, but by 1985, even guys, in places like Le Suer, Minnesota were dressing like the TV cop duo.

And anyone who was anyone in the music and entertainment world wanted to be a guest star on the show.

Bruce Willis played the role of a gun dealer just as his career was taking off, and Willie Nelson played the part of a vigilante Texas Ranger long after he had recorded countless hits. Comedian Chris Rock had a small role in an episode and actor Ed O'Neil played a sleazy porn producer on *Miami Vice* before he hit it big on *Married...with Children.*

Few TV shows have influenced pop culture as *Miami Vice* did, and with the way that TV programming has become so decentralized today, we will probably never see it happen again.

1980s Pop Culture Quiz

1. _____ was one of the music styles that influenced 1980s fashion.

2. The hit show *Miami Vice* was on what TV network?

3. What year did MTV first go on the air?

4. Other than Levi, what were the cool name-brand jeans in the '80s?

5. The *Afterschool Special* appeared on what TV network?

6. _____ was Johnny Carson's trusty sidekick for the entirety of his show.

7. What year did the home video game industry crash?

8. Young people often called their portable cassette players _____ in the '80s.

9. _____ and _____ were the star actors on *Miami Vice*.

10. The Intellivision video game console was made by which company?

Answers

1. Punk; new wave; heavy metal; rap/hip hop; country

2. NBC

3. 1981

4. Guess

5. ABC

6. Ed McMahon

7. 1983

8. Boom box; ghetto blaster

9. Don Johnson and Philip Michael Thomas

10. Mattel

Did You Know?

- You probably remember actor David Hasselhoff from the sci-fi TV series *Knight Rider*, which ran from 1982 to 1986, but did you know Hasselhoff also has a long recording career and that he is popular in Germany? That's right, the "Hass" even performed his 1988 hit song "Looking for Freedom" in front of what was left of the Berlin Wall after it was torn down.

- If you were a kid or had kids in the '80s, chances are you remember KangaRoos. What were KangaRoos? They were a brand of sneakers that all the kids wanted by the mid-'80s. And if you were really cool, you got a pair of Roos with Velcro straps!

- One of the results of the diverse music and clothing styles in the 1980s was the emergence of new youth subcultures. The punk and skinhead subcultures, which originated in England, became popular in the US, as did the "metalhead", hip hop, and "urban cowboy" subcultures.

- To cater to these varied musical tastes, MTV developed late-night shows for specific music genres. Alternative music fans could tune into

120 Minutes to see the latest Cure video, metal fans got their fix with *The Headbangers Ball*, and hip-hop aficionados had *Yo! MTV Raps*.

- Do you remember the Atari 5200 game console? If not, you're not alone. The Atari 5200 was released in 1982 as an upgrade to the 2600, meant to challenge some of the other game consoles at the time that had better graphics, but the video game collapse of 1983 killed the idea, and the system was discontinued in 1984.

1980s Science

Space Shuttle Columbia Launches

On April 12, 1981, the world watched as NASA made another bold scientific leap forward when it successfully launched from the Kennedy Space Center in Merritt Island, Florida, and landed two days later on an airstrip at Edwards Airforce Base in Edwards, California. It was important because it was the first vehicle capable of entering space and returning to Earth intact.

Space shuttles were now able to be reused, and they could land on conventional airstrips instead of crashing in the ocean like previous rockets.

During the 1980s, NASA built four shuttles — Columbia, Challenger, Discovery, and Enterprise — and the fifth shuttle in 1992, Endeavor, which combined to fly 135 missions from 1981 until the program ended in 2011.

The Space Shuttle program was a source of pride for NASA and the United States and helped spur a renewed international interest in space. The Space Shuttles brought astronauts out into space to work with cosmonauts on the Mir Space Station as well as helping to launch countless satellites and the Hubble Space Telescope.

Since NASA became so reliant on the Space Shuttle Program by the mid-'80s, the *Challenger* disaster set the program back but didn't end it. On September 29, 1988, the Space Shuttle *Discovery* made its maiden flight and became the first Space Shuttle to go into space after the *Challenger* disaster.

ARPANET Goes National

You may remember a few years ago when Al Gore said he invented the internet. No one really quite knows why or how he came up with that statement, since the internet as we know it was the culmination of several projects that were finally made public in 1981.

It all started in 1969 with the Advanced Research Projects Agency (ARPA) of the US Defense Department as the Advanced Research Projects Agency Network (ARPANET). The ARPANET was *the* internet in the 1970s, but there were no dating sites, no eBay, and certainly no porn!

The purpose was for military and intelligence agencies to send information instantaneously, but almost immediately the possibilities for civilian research were cited, so in 1981, it was expanded under funding from the National Science Foundation. For the first few years of the '80s, access to the Net was still restricted to universities, but by the middle of the decade, the internet as we know it today was being built on the technology of ARPANET.

Finally, in 1989, English scientist Tim Berners-Lee took all his knowledge of computer networks to propose the idea of a worldwide computer network that would be easy for everyone to access. He called his idea the World Wide Web and by 1990 it became a reality.

So, if anyone can claim to be the inventor of the internet, it would by Tim Berners-Lee, although he'd probably be the first to tell you that it was a long process in which many scientists contributed.

Halley's Comet Makes an Appearance

Humans have known about comets since the dawn of time and every literate culture throughout history has written about them. Comets have been a source of mystery, fear, and awe, but perhaps none more so than Halley's Comet.

Do you get a chance to see Halley's Comet the last time it passed through our inner solar system in 1986?

It was definitely a big event around the world, with governments, private businesses, and individuals arranging comet watch parties. Schools had special programs to educate kids about the science and history of the comet, and just about every time you put on the TV or radio, there was something on about Halley's Comet.

History, pop culture, and science all collided in 1986 when it came to Halley's Comet.

So why was it such a big deal?

Well, since it only passes close enough to Earth for it to be visible every 75 years, chances are you'll only have one chance to see it in your lifetime, so that's kind of a big deal.

And then there's the science behind it.

Halley's Comet was the first comet in history to be photographed and tracked from space. The Soviets sent two unmanned space probes named Vega 1 and Vega 2 to observe the comet, which was followed by unmanned observation probes sent by the European and Japanese space agencies.

The Americans planned to send a Space Shuttle, but then the *Challenger* disaster happened.

Haley's Comet was first observed with a telescope from Earth in January 1985, and by late 1986, it would be gone until 2061. The 1985-86 viewing of Halley's Comet was generally not incredibly good due to a combination of it being on the opposite side of the Sun for most of its trip and heavy light pollution throughout the Earth. The best views were in rural areas with binoculars and telescopes.

Well, maybe your grandkids and great-grandkids will get a better view in '61.

A Poisonous Lake

Have you ever heard of a limnic eruption? If you haven't, don't feel bad since it's a pretty rare occurrence and geologists are the only people who know much about them. But if you were following the news much in the mid-1980s then you probably remember hearing about the devastation that a limnic eruption can cause.

On August 21, 1986, a limnic eruption in Lake Nyos in northwestern Cameroon left 1,746 people dead and even more livestock dead and inedible.

Of course, you're probably wondering, what is a limnic eruption, and how did it happen on Lake Nyos? Well, the answer to the first part is actually pretty easy, even with scientific jargon, but the second part is somewhat of a mystery.

A limnic eruption is when carbon dioxide (CO_2) discharges from a large body of water and forms a deadly cloud of gas. Since CO_2 is heavier than air, after the cloud forms, it descends on the surrounding area with a deadly effect, which is exactly what happened at Lake Nyos.

Up to a million tons of gas was released, killing some people almost instantaneously, but inflicting a longer, more painful death on others that usually involved paralysis and suffocating to death.

Scientists still don't know exactly what triggered the limnic eruption at Lake Nyos. It could have been a volcano, a landslide, excess cool waters on one side of the lake, or an earthquake.

The Lake Nyos disaster did have some positive consequences, though. Scientists were able to observe a limnic eruption in action, so today they know the warning signs to look for in future events. Scientists have also developed pumping systems that can extract CO_2 from lakes via pipes.

The Father of DNA Profiling

Thanks to forensic police shows, both fictional and documentary, there's almost no chance that you don't know that deoxyribonucleic acid (DNA) is the code that contains each of our unique "genetic fingerprints." You probably also know from these shows that DNA is used to catch criminals.

But DNA profiling is also used to determine paternity, can isolate genetic diseases, and can be utilized in hundreds of other medical and scientific applications. Although the knowledge of DNA has been around since the 1800s, the process by which DNA can be connected to a specific person - DNA profiling - is a discovery of the 1980s, thanks to the work of Englishman Alec Jeffreys.

Jeffreys earned a PhD from the University of Amsterdam in genetics, but it was while he was working at the University of Leicester in 1984 that he made one of the greatest leaps forward in biological science in history.

Before Jeffreys, biologists and geneticists knew that different species had different DNA, but they didn't know that different *individuals* had unique DNA profiles.

Jeffreys knew that this was potentially a momentous discovery, but he had to put his theory to the test. In 1985, he got the chance when he profiled the DNA of a boy in an immigration case. Jeffrey's process proved that the boy was related to a family living in the UK, allowing the boy to stay in the country but foreshadowing even bigger implications.

Then, in 1987, Jeffreys first used DNA profiling in the case of Colin Pitchfork, who was a suspect in the murder and rape of a girl in 1983, and another in 1986. Jeffreys profiled the DNA of both victims as well as body fluids on them left by the killer.

The DNA profile of the killer matched Colin Pitchfork!

The case made little news outside of the UK, but within ten years, DNA profiling was used by police departments around the world. Thanks to Alec Jeffreys, countless killers have been taken off the streets, innocent people have been freed from prison, lost family members have been reunited, and new treatments for deadly and debilitating diseases have been developed.

It's no wonder that Jeffreys was knighted in 1994 for his contributions not just to his country but to the entire world.

You Know Why They Called Them Bricks

Before the 1980s, if you were an important person always on the go but who needed to always be available to your customers and contacts, you had a car phone. You may find this hard to believe, but the car phone was first available in 1946 through Motorola. It didn't become a big thing, however, until the 1980s.

Car phones used radio technology, where calls would be routed through a service, which in the early years was manned by human operators.

But in 1984, a new wave of communications technology splashed over the world when Motorola introduced its DynaTAC 8000X. The DynaTAC had truly little in common with the smartphones of today, other than both making phone calls, but without the former, we never would have had the latter.

The DynaTAC was the culmination of decades of research by engineers such as Martin Cooper, who invented the first handheld cellular phone. The cell phone was distinct from the car phone because it used cellular technology and had to operate on a system known as the Advanced Mobile Phone System (AMPS), which allowed users to directly connect to other phones in the system or landline phones.

Do you remember the big rush to buy the DynaTAC?

Me neither, because it never happened. Although the DynaTAC was popular with some business executives and other influential people, unless you were Donald Trump, you probably didn't own one. The cost was a whopping $4,000, and the bulky things took about ten hours to charge and only gave you about a half-hour of talk time per charge!

And then there was the size.

The DynaTAC was about nine inches tall when placed on its base and weighed nearly three pounds. The phone's size and look earned it the nickname the "brick," but Cooper and Motorola had the last laugh as DynaTAC sold fairly well, at least relative to its high price, opening the door for its later, smaller, and more inexpensive successors.

1980s Science Quiz

1. When a lake shifts, releasing poisonous carbon dioxide, the process is known as a _____.

2. Halley's Comet was last visible on Earth in what year?

3. _____ was the scientist who discovered DNA profiling.

4. ARPANET expanded to civilian use in what year?

5. The first handheld cellular phone was invented by _____.

6. Besides Columbia and Challenger, what was the name of another NASA Space Shuttle that made missions into space?

7. DNA profiling was first used in a criminal case in what year?

8. Lake Nyos is located in what African nation?

9. The DynaTAC 8000X cellphone first went on the market in what year?

10. ARPANET is an abbreviation of _____.

Answers

1. Limnic eruption

2. 1985-1986

3. Alec Jeffreys

4. 1981

5. Martin Cooper

6. Atlantis; Discovery; Endeavor

7. 1987

8. Cameroon

9. 1984

10. Advanced Research Projects Agency Network

Did You Know?

- The Soviet Union built a Space Shuttle they called Buran (Blizzard) in the 1980s. It only flew one unmanned orbit in 1988 before the Soviet Union collapsed and the program was scrapped.

- Lake Nyos is a crater lake that sits next to an inactive volcano. A volcanic dam holds in the waters of the lake, although the wall is weakening, which threatens villages in Cameroon and nearby Nigeria with flooding.

- The Advanced Mobile Phone System was the primary cell phone system throughout most of the world until the 2000s. It operated on the analog signal so when most countries moved to digital systems, it was eliminated.

- George Wesley has the dubious honor of being the first American convicted of murder through DNA profiling. In 1988, he was convicted in a New York court of murdering a woman named Helen Kendrick. Blood on Kendrick's shirt was matched to Wesley's DNA profile, sealing the case against him, and establishing the use of DNA profiling in American courtrooms.

- Halley's Comet nucleus is about nine miles by five miles in size, which is relatively small for a comet. It's Halley's *coma*, all the diffuse gasses around it, including the tail, that make it so visible. Halley's Comet's coma is more than 62,000 miles across, giving it an impressive look in the night sky.

CONCLUSION

Thanks for taking this trivia ride with us through the '50s, '60s, '70s, and '80s - you no doubt had some fun on your trip down memory lane and maybe even learned a few things along the way! I'm sure as you read each chapter you remembered other events, trends, and scientific achievements that weren't included in our quiz, which only means that we've at least partially accomplished our goal by helping you keep your mind sharp.

As for the fun, I'm sure you had plenty! After all, as was mentioned in the introduction, this quiz book was meant to be read with your friends and family. You can pick and choose chapters, or subsections of the chapters, according to the people you're with.

So, remember, the next time you're drinking some coffee with your friends and the conversation gets a little boring, or Canasta just isn't doing it anymore, bust out *Trivia for Seniors* and see how much you and your friends remember about your youth in the '50s and '60s.

Or the next time your kids come to visit with their kids, and you want to get your grandkids away from their phones and tablets, challenge your children to a face-off over the '70s and '80s trivia. I guarantee that your kids will answer the challenge and their kids will get a kick out of watching their parents and grandparents match trivia wits.

Whichever way that you use this book, just have fun, and remember that you've lived in some fascinating times — but the best is yet to come!

MORE BOOKS BY BILL O'NEILL

I hope you enjoyed this book
and learned something new.

Please feel free to check out some
of my previous books on Amazon.

Made in the USA
Las Vegas, NV
27 November 2021

35229812R00105